...house of the rising mug...

...rocky-o...

America Star Books
Frederick, Maryland

Softcover 9781682905296
PUBLISHED BY AMERICA STAR BOOKS, LLLP
www.americastarbooks.pub
Frederick, Maryland

...grey kinda world...

little is to be known

yet the tone is reverberating

off the walls and it

sounds magnificent

...simple...silent...solo...

to the depth of the

granite and the feeling

of the concrete

beneath this trench

within this breath

the atmosphere within

the atmosphere

the grey within the

grey

of this kinda world

...

influences...

past...present...future...

places...sam goody, think coffee,
and that little church i found in the bahamas...

sights...'the window', 'the river', and 'the
curtain'...

events...katrina relief, 'little me' happenings,
and playing ski-ball in times square...

special event...seeing my baby thru her cancer
battle,
and seeing the beautiful support of those
around her...

authors...oscar wilde, william golding,
and 'prolific props' to stephen king...

journalists...rob corich, alan clayson,
and les davidson...

songwriters...david bowie, bill nelson, and
roger waters...

singer/songwriter friends...linda dunn, and
christine kane...

friends...alan muir, and lenni matula...

...special voices...henry diltz, maura o'connell,
and edward hopper...

...and...

(...and voices spoken here...dorothy rocker,
jazz carpenter,
watchman, and dust...)

***

and, my favorite 'room' mate, my angel carol
(puma warrior)...

and, of course, the holy spirit,
my favorite 'soul' mate...

...peace always...

TABLE OF CONTEXT

...prologue...

...arabica cadabrica...

—

that first cup in the morning

after a long long night...

that first pop of a new tin coffee can lid

that makes the world seem right...

the arcma that hits your senses

that's sent right down to your soul...

the scoop, the brew, the auto-drip thru

of straight black as black as coal...

the pour, the release, the thirst, the heat

the tracking of glorious splendor

the eyes that are closed, the rush to your toes

the feeling of god's own nectar...

that first cup in the morning

that melts the mind from stone

god may have turned the water to wine

but he left the coffee alone...

...new york city...
—

there's an aching feeling inside...
trapped inside my mind
and i'll find it on the 'L' line above...
waiting for a train...

blinded by the moonlight
shining off this plastic world
i'm all alone...

'cept for the bench i've come to call my own...

the sirens scream
and the lights burn right around me
the soundtrack of the city reeks...
as the voices lay silent still...

the recognition is incoherent
as the night has its way...

what can i say...

what can i say...

the night will always have its way

with me...

here in new york city...

...chapter one...

...mug shot...

—

with the moon barely out of sight, and a cigarette dangerously close to setting her bed on fire, dorothy rocker groggily rises, not unlike a phoenix from the flame...a little burnt for wear...

but, once again, she is only awakening from her crypt to answer her phone, which, one day, she will remember to shut off before she goes to bed...if she can remember going to bed in the first place...

but she knew that, only one person would dare call her up this early...

...actual two...

one...a telemarketer, that, although just doing their job, seriously deserves a dial tone faster than a republican running for the white house...

or two...jazz carpenter...

jazz knew dorothy didn't like mornings...why else would he call this early...

planning his demise, dorothy answered the phone...

"no, no, no...", she screamed into the phone, while flicking the mile-long ash from her cigarette...

"no what?...", replied jazz, knowing exactly what she was saying 'no' to...

then there was just silence...all jazz could hear was someone hocking a morning loogie in the background, and closing the bathroom door...

...and he smiled...

...time and a word...

—

time is a bandit that steals away while you're blinking...from one moment to the next, it's subtle, but it's there...like fear, born of a primal extinct, time is bred from that same volition...but, in time's case, the lack thereof cries havoc when there is none...

time for dorothy has been wearing thin, as her 'vacation minutes' were dwindling down to a precious few...and with so much espresso left to manifest...

she is fortunate that her job doesn't require a nine-to-five straight-jacket, however, some days it's a 24/7 way of life...

and once again, just as she hung up her phone, it rang...

"hey dot...ya' don't have to pick up, it's just me, jazz...listen...i got us a gig at whole lotta books for this thursday nite...they had a last minute cancellation...the author thomas blake was supposed to read from his new book, but something happened and he had to cancel...i didn't even know he finally came out with his second book, but anyway, it starts at..."...beep...

and then the tape cut off...

dorothy sat and thought to herself..."man...when is that guy gonna learn how to speak faster..."

so, reluctantly, she picked up the phone to call him back...

...and when jazz answered, dorothy flew into her usual diatribe..."what's the matter with you... are you a new yorker or what...ya' talk like your from bumbletown, ya' mook...get to the point and move on...i haven't got all day ya' know, i'm a busy woman...and i certainly don't have time to waste listening to your obtuse ramblings when there's coffee to drink..."

jazz took a pause..."ya' done yet?..."

dorothy took a pause herself, thought a moment and said..."yea...i think so...but later on i got about twenty minutes worth of stuff i've been saving since new years..."

...take blake...

—

taking a beat, jazz wisely ignored her and continued...

"well...", he said formally..."i don't know how much you heard but, we got a reading gig, this thursday at 'whole lotta books', starting at 7pm..."...

dorothy wisely asked "which location?..."

"oh yea...", jazz responded off-guard..."the 8th street store...up by 5th..."

"what time..." she asked..."seven...", he replied...
"what time..." she asked..."seven...", he replied...
"what time..." she asked...he refused to answer...

"seriously...", she continued..."how are we gonna work this out...is this just gonna be stuff from my book, or you wanna show off some of dust's stuff...i also got some stuff here from watchman that i would love to spotlight as well..."

"i kinda figured...", he smirked..."...actually, i really didn't figure on anything, but, we could do that, that would be cool..."

dorothy looked at her phone like he could actually see her expression...

"you don't have the faintest idea what you're doing,
do you?"...she mocked...

"listen...", he came back explaining..."i'm only one
man, stop beating me up already...all i did was
talk to them about something in the future...hell,
your book isn't even out yet, don't bite my head
off, they're just being nice and letting us have this
slot..."

"well, thank you thomas blake for canceling...",
dorothy signed sarcastically...

...demitasse in the details...

—

dorothy continued her conversation with jazz a little further, until she couldn't take anymore... "listen...i'll try to get a hold of watchman later on today...i'll have to talk to him before i can agree to anything..."

jazz, feeling confident by dorothy's response simply said..."cool...let me know when you know...o.k.?..."

"yea...no problem...", dorothy replied...

"thanx hun...sorry for disturbing you", jazz said sincerely...

dorothy just sighed..."yea, yea...love you too...", and with that, she hung up the phone and fell back on her bed...

unfortunately for dorothy, her tiredness wasn't equal to her concern about getting in touch with watchman, and having to figure out everything in just a few days...

she figured her best bet was to head back to 'brewed indigo' and maybe she'd be lucky enough to catch sight of him...since he had no phone or address, this was not gonna be the easiest task of her day, but it did put a bit of a smile on her face when she thought about getting watchman his own cell phone, so that she could contact him easier...she figured that, with everything coming up, it was probably gonna be essential, and she would gladly throw on a few minutes every now and then to keep it going...and he was gonna have to plug it in every once in a while, so, maybe he could do that at the coffee shop, but better to let him just leave it at her apartment to charge up...

at this point, dorothy's mind was reeling, and knowing she wasn't going to get any rest, she instead made a bee-line to the coffee pot, which was already on and hot, and where she figured she could pull a headline out by drinking herself into an imploded suicide...

'death by caffination', she thought, as she tumbled towards her mug...

...and after about twenty cups, she hit the shower, and promptly fell asleep standing up...

...first do no bodily harm...

—

while in the shower, dorothy's mind was reeling even further, now focused on the reading night, considering what pieces she would want to read, along with which ones she definitely would not...

and something even more unusual happened to dorothy that she hadn't experienced before...the need for a pen...

soaking wet, all she could think about were new pieces, words streaming in her brain, and here she was without anything to write it down with...

she quickly jumped out of the shower, not even bothering to shut off the water...she grabbed a towel and ran over to her desk, grabbing a pad, which now had splashes of water and soap upon it, and tried writing down what she was hearing...

she tried and realized that 'trying' just wouldn't cut it...

"oh crap..."...she said, throwing the pad back down on the desk..."it was so good too..."

she slowly walked back into the bathroom to shut off the shower, then promptly walked back into the living room to light up another smoke...

she sat down, still considerably wet, but not truly caring...she took a long, deep drag, tilted her head back, and blew a column of smoke up in the air that either signified her annoyance, or simply meant that a new pope had been elected...

she thought to herself...”so that’s how watchman does it...”, to which, she took another drag, and closed her eyes, leaving one slightly open, eyeing the pen and pad on her desk...just in case...

...ex-communication...

—

after drying off, and polishing off a full pot of coffee and a half-pack of smokes, she threw on some sweats and sat quietly in the dark...

glancing over at her picture of amelia earhart, she felt like amelia herself was staring at her...

"i know!...I know!", dorothy cried out, as she slumped further into her chair...

amelia remained silent...

dorothy's mind however, was anything but silent...

she looked around at the brick walls and the ceiling and the floor, and the coffee machine and everything else that she could look at, other than her typewriter...

not that she had anything against her typewriter... this was her tried-n-true rusted old friend that has seen her thru alot of verbiage over the years, and now was not a time for alienation...

but she knew...she just knew that...something was just...off...

she tried remembering what she had thought about in the shower, and slowly grabbed a piece of paper...she rolled it in, sat a little straighter, and began hitting keys...

she wasn't writing, barely even typing...no...she was just hitting keys...

'utter nonsense', she thought at first, convincing herself that writing was a fool's errand at best, but, after a few more sips and deep breaths, she at least now tried to 'recite' what she had previously thought, and then type it down, to, at least, have something...

after she was thru, she read it...

it was a little like what she had originally thought, but...it wasn't quite right...

...divided by...

—

she read it again and again, and, the more she read it, the more she hated it...

not just disliked, not just unacceptable...this was hate...in its purest form...

it didn't flow. it wasn't exactly the same words, kinda the same meaning, but...

dorothy grabbed the paper with ferocity, pulled it out of the typewriter with velocity, and crumpled it up, mumbling "crap, crap, crap" to herself...

she threw it in the trash can next to her desk, and couldn't help thinking about a copy machine...how copies, no matter how good they may look, never come out as good as the original...

she realized the same thing about writing...

after all these years of being a 'professional' writer, she always kinda felt that she still had something to learn, and she guessed that this was finally it...

it never bothered her before, when she felt something sucked, and she would later write, "...this sucks.."

but this was different...this was a sensory feeling that needed to be expressed when it needed to be expressed, not just after a billion cups of coffee and enough smokes to rival the chicago fire...

she, for a moment, felt enlightened, envisioned, a revelation in her mind and spirit...

and then...she shook her head in disgust, said angrily to herself, "what am i babbling about", and lit another cigarette...

she laid her head back against the chair, blew a ring of smoke into the air, and reminded herself of who she was and where she was...

...downtown brownstone...

—

walking around the postage stamp of her apartment, she was spying anything and everything that she felt would inspire her...

she thought of putting on some nice music to maybe get her in the mood for something good...

she thought about watching some news to piss her off, and maybe that would bring out something even better...

like most writers, dorothy knows that, you always write the best stuff when you are mad...or sad... but never happy...words don't do happy well...

so she started to think of everything that she didn't like...drunk drivers, reality shows, republicans, you name it...

...and she found herself getting mad...fake mad...

she was trying too hard...after a while, she just started laughing at the absurdity of it all...

"it'll come when it comes", she told herself and any spirit that may have been listening to her...after all, there was a part of her that perhaps thought that, maybe if 'somebody' or 'something' was listening, they may want to throw her a bone and pony something up in her brain to write about...

but there was nothing...

"thanx a lot...", she said with the utmost sarcasm she could muster...

and with that, she crushed her cigarette right down to its filter, made sure her coffee pot was off, blew amelia a kiss, and proceeded to go back to sleep...

...lost snore of the rotogravure...

—

while lying on her cot, she stared at the ceiling...

she really couldn't fall asleep...actually didn't want to...

and with all the stuff going on inside her head that she didn't want to think about, well...that was just much more company than she wanted to keep...

she knew her rent was due soon and, although she had the money to pay for it, barely, she did have to think about where watchman might have been at that moment, and where he spent the night before...

also...the thought of jazz laid on her mind as well, the whole thing about the book reading and everything...she didn't really need that kind of pressure...or at least, annoyance...

but...on the other hand, it would be kinda cool to get some of dust's stuff out there...and perhaps even watchman's, if he wouldn't mind...and, to be truthful, getting her stuff read wouldn't be bad either...

as she contemplated further she easily understood that, getting it done wasn't the problem...it was having to do it that was the issue...

...and she really didn't want to do it...not at this moment anyway, but, she knew that when it came around to it, she would probably fall into place with it...

and thinking about all this stuff right now kept her mind off of the real issue at hand...what amelia "said" to her...

now, of course, she knows that it's just a photo, an old one at that, and that dear amelia is no longer around to actually 'have a conversation with her' in her living room, but, as for inspiration, that's a whole 'nother story...

and when amelia tells you that there's need to be more, well...there needs to be more...

dorothy knew that her own stuff was missing something...just by comparison, she felt something lacking...but...she didn't know what...

...topping off the bottomless cup...

—

she rolled over and reached for some of her papers...

she started reading piece by piece, to see if she could unravel the mystery...

she would read, and turn to the next page saying... 'well, that wasn't too bad...', and then begin to read the next page...

after she got thru about a dozen or so, she got up and went back into the living and made a beeline for the coffee pot once again...

she had to start a new pot, since she totally obliterated the last one, and, when she started scooping out the grounds, she went into some kind of 'auto-drip' mode...

she just stared at the grounds, as they lay in the filter...

she went to get some water, and filled up the well, only to continue staring into another zone...

she clicked on the machine and proceeded to walk over to her typewriter, still dazed...

she put in a fresh piece of paper and started away, not even thinking about what keys she was hitting...

before, when she was just 'hitting keys', it was an exercise in futility, but this was more than that... this was writing, not even typing...

typing would be too pedestrian a word for what she was going thru...

and when she was thru, somehow she knew it... even though she had no clue what she had actually written...

she pulled out the paper, and instead of crumpling it up this time, she sat back, took a brief moment, and then read it for the first time...

...birthright...

—

as i measure out my coffee grounds, i feel my life as unspecific as the eye on which i make these rounds...

and as the hot water flows and bursts the dam, i wonder who i am, and where...

i don't care for my location, although i've seen worse on my destinations, i assure you...

but the brew is only a temporary cure for the real coffeehouse my heart desires to stop in right now...

don't get me wrong, i love this apartment...but it's just a compartment to a muse this side of the door...

it's what's on the other side that makes me chide like this for sure...but still...

i get to heaven most every chance i get, but ya' can't always get what you want, so they say, and if this is what i need, so be it for now, it's o.k...for a place upon a license plate does not negate who i am or how...

the certificate upon my birth is my worth...cut
the bark and count the streets...and watch the
subway slide on thru to the true brew instead of
these facsimile beats that i'm currently perking...

but at least it's something...

...one may smile and smile...

—

she read it and re-read it a dozen times, finding something new each time she read it...

there were bits that were definitely personal, some poetic, and some just outright blatant...

but...like the last line said...it was something...

and...when dorothy looked over at the photo of amelia, she seemed to have a smile on her face...

not that that smile wasn't always in the photo, but...this may have been the first time dorothy actually noticed it...

...and now...

—

with a bit of a smile on her own face, dorothy finally got dressed and made her way downstairs to the streets that knew her all too well, and a direction that was becoming equally familiar...

making her way to 'brewed indigo', dorothy kept her eyes peeled, hoping to catch a glimpse of her long-haired friend...

she passed by 'vinylocity', one of the few record stores left in the city, and for a moment, she thought to herself...'what am i doing?...where is my album on the wall?...'

that's a dream she always had, made minor strides back in the day to achieving, but lately, the typewriter has been her more constant companion, rather than a mic and amp...

but it doesn't stop her from believing that, one day...maybe...

and while her mind drifted, she accidentally walked into a subway post, bruising her ribcage, but more importantly bruising her composure, turning around with a glance that said...'...what are you looking at?...'

...but nobody was looking...

and by this time, she made her way to the coffeehouse, and, while standing in front, rubbing her side and waiting to catch watchman, she decided that she may as well go in and imbibe 'the nectar of the gods' while she was waiting...

and now, while focusing on her previous biting pieces of spit and vinegar, she couldn't help but also think about her 'missteps' in life, opportunities she may have missed, those moments when she just didn't feel 'dorothy' enough...

this was a feeling she was not at all pleased with, usually settling for a 'rougher' exterior, with an interior to match...

...but like she contemplated earlier, this morning was definitely not the usual...

...land of the free...

—

she gently moved her java out of the way to place her pen and pad on the table...

she felt that, if the spirit was gonna hit her again to write, she was gonna be ready this time...

and so, she waited...and waited...and waited...

...and, at one point, she actually felt like her soul was trying to push something out, like a woman delivering a baby...(a frightening thought to dorothy...)

she finally gave up, putting down her pen and getting up to get another cup of joe...

and, of course, while she was waiting on line, and waiting, and waiting, inspiration struck as it usually does, and she ran back to her table to jot down these words...

"...america is a great country...americans don't deserve it..."

she didn't exactly take in what she wrote, but just the fact that she wrote it was a sigh of relief for her...

she smiled and walked back to the line, which was now even longer, but she didn't care...

for her...'dorothy' was back...

...whaddya hear whaddya say...

—

when she got back to her table, before she could even put her several cups of coffee down, her phone rang...

she looked and noticed that it was jazz, so she flipped it open and started speaking before he could...

"no, i haven't seen him yet...yes, i'm at brewed indigo now...no, i have no idea what his answer is going to be...yes, i'll ask him...no, i haven't hit my eighteenth cup yet...(pause)...any other questions..."

"well hello to you too...", jazz said with the sarcastic response that only knowing dorothy for so long could inspire...

"whaddya want?...", she hastily asked...

"why must you always be this way?...", jazz calmly expressed, to which dorothy replied...

"didn't you hear...i'm back"...

there was silence on both ends of the phone...

"anyway, seriously, what's up?...", dorothy said in a more acclimating tone...

jazz, responding in kind, said..."listen..."

now, when dorothy hears jazz start a sentence with 'listen', her ears perk up like a doberman pincher... "...i'm listening..." she said with anticipation...

"just listen", he replied sharply..."anyway, i was talking with jeremiah kent, you know, the guy from worx radio...he loves doing all those book readings and author interviews and stuff, and i just thought..."

dorothy stopped him in mid sentence..."doesn't take a genius to figure out where you're going with this..."

...jazzercise...

—

jazz, ignoring dorothy's excuse for wit, continued to inform her about the idea of her going on his show..."he's really keen about the idea..."

"keen?...did you just say keen?...", dorothy exclaimed...

"yea...what's wrong with 'keen'?...", jazz asked hypothetically...

dorothy, not passing up this question, hypothetical or otherwise, came back with..."where do i begin?..."

once again, there was silence on both ends of the phone...

dorothy decided to break the détente by asking... "are you sure you're a new yorker?..."

she wasn't kidding...

jazz countered with..."ya' wanna see my birth certificate, not like that phony one you had made up that still says you're only twenty-five..."

"thirty-three, wise guy...and that was just a reminder to myself that i'm only as old as i feel..."

"well thank you for that eternal wise one...let me get out my fortune cookie so i can stamp it in..."

after a brief pause from both sides, jazz finally said..."so...do you wanna do it or what?...", to which dorothy grinned..."what?..."

"you know what", jazz sighed..."the radio show..."

"do i 'wanna' do it?...", dorothy pondered..."no... will i do it...i'll think about it..."

"well don't think too long...i need to call him back tomorrow...", jazz commented...

"alright...i'll let you know...", dorothy said regaining her civility, "...so, how is everything else going?..."

...unsettled rust from a previous cup...

—

dorothy eventually finished up her conversation with jazz, never giving him a definitive answer on anything...

she closed her phone, and looked around at the various customers that were sitting at tables next to hers...

there were some travelers, who seemed foreign to her...and, when she heard them speak, their accents did sound like they may have been austrian...'...or somewhere in that region...'...dorothy thought...

another table had this very pretty young girl, young by dorothy's standards, which was anyone under forty, who was, of course on her laptop typing away...

"the next dorothy rocker", dorothy thought to herself, as she furiously tried to notice what the girl was drinking...

when the young lady removed the cup from her lips, dorothy could see a little white foam still on her upper lip, as though there was whipped cream in whatever she was inhaling...

dorothy just shrugged, and with a harrumph said..."definitely NOT the next dorothy..."

this made her smile, as she felt there could only be one in the first place, and young people today where getting away with too damn much anyway...

'they're taking over the job market, they can't spell, they certainly can't write...', and this diatribe went on in dorothy's mind for about another twenty minutes...

after a pause to breathe, dorothy took a moment to ponder...

'yes...', she thought...'...and there's still a lot that needs to be written...'

and with that...

...private little heaven...

—

alone...but never alone...

the paper-thin walls let in all i need to know...

and it shows...beyond the depth of anything humanity has to offer...

and i can get it for you wholesale...

whatever you see, whatever you hear...in the heart of every

dream...the corners seem to mock every go round... their chance is

coming and their day is eventful, but we of ye born-n-bred are never

resentful...

the bed of the city's pavement...the certain soil that grows in the

basement...enough to chainlink a fence...at whose expense...

this world unto its own worth...this private little
heaven in hell on

earth...

...fandango...

—

like an ocean in a cup
that is spilled upon the floor
the souls are lining up
and they're waiting at the door

how many people cry...how many children die
and how many wonder why
and simply stand there breathing

like a hurricane of peace
that still needs to be
the hurricane intended
even when it's cast to sea

how many people see...how many don't believe
how many hear the screams
but simply stand there grieving

how many people cry...how many children die
how many wonder why
but simply stand there breathing...

like an ocean in a cup
that is spilled upon the floor
the souls are lining up
and there's bound to be some more

how many people care...how many really dare
how many simply swear
at all the children needing...

how many close their eyes...how many don't realize
how many sacrifice
for all of those left bleeding

how many people cry...how many children die
how many wonder why
but simply stand there breathing...

...still like coffee...
—

like coffee

caught within the rain

tempered by the frozen winds

sheltered by the cup surrounding

held together by its substance

a weakening

but not a deafening

still straight black

still strong

still like coffee

caught within the rain

...red herring...

—

longing to see god is not enough

tying down the tent before it blows
and it's all about you

tendering exchange of monies owed
there's a new movie coming out to

fire roasting golden brown
life can be so pleasant sometimes

bosses stressing over lost and found
feet are cold...neck it bends
gazing at your vitamins

so tired...so tired...

enjoying the aftertaste of your morning cup
longing to see god is not enough

...broken country...

—

this is a broken country

two points of view sharing one land

two views 180-degrees in-between

two statutes of power...

those who have it

and those who don't...

news that can spin an election

news that matters who repeats it

we need to separate this land

if we ever expect to agree

for our disagreements

this is a broken country...

...skunks-n-roses...

—

what is it with all these celebrity perfumes?...do people actually think

they'll be rich and famous if they wear this stuff, like smelling like

somebody famous will change who they are?...

and what's with the fragrances they choose... everything smells like a

friggin' garden...i hate perfume...i hate roses...at least, smelling them...

i'm waiting for the celebrity that has the guts to put out a fragrance that

smells like skunk...

i like skunk...

coffee wouldn't be bad either...a nice espresso scent to start the day...

maybe i'll just have to do it myself...

...none like a magnet...

—

new york angels
out on the street
a foreign land
but a familiar beat
their p.a. is damaged
so no one can hear
their message triumphant
but not often clear
the wheels they keep rolling
the trash is still reaching
the motor is climbing
the night air is breaching
the weather controlling
the air is still stagnant
there's plenty to do here
but none like a magnet
those old new york angels
on pavement redundant
their bags are all packed
with no mission accomplished
their hopes are all rendered
their eyes are all closed
their rags are in tatters
as everyone knows
their speaker is subtle
their voices are loud
but none like a magnet
is found in the crowd

...parability...

—

a man comes upon a hole, that's 45 feet deep...

nobody likes the hole, so he begins to fill it in...

after four years, he has filled 30 feet of the hole, but hasn't finished yet...

nobody thanks him for filling in over half the hole...

everybody now just blames him that they have a 15 foot hole...

they forget that he wasn't the one who dug the hole in the first place...

he was just trying to help...

...brew zipline and the mugs of incinea...

—

sending out an s.o.s.
the planet's now in mass distress
the kingdom has been overthrown by fear

the forces that are gathering
are wiping out their enemy
with one objective that's become quite clear

their agenda all along
was to take over the nation
and soon they would be strong
over hints and allegations
and their tentacles would reach
beyond the barrier to breach
total control
of hearts and souls

the little band that would resist
had no course but the evidence
that once there stood a mighty land below

what once was known as jah vahroole
has now become an evil tool
by those who stood in favor of the gold

their position all along
was to wipe out every truth
to tear apart the right from wrong
and set in place their view
and their grip would let the blood
run thru fingers just like mud
'til total acceptance
of their insurrection

replying to their s.o.s.
a voice reached out into their mess
and promised them that he would do his best...

...pinballs on the playground...

yes...she was back...and still quite amused over that last piece she wrote...

dorothy tucked up her pen and paper, as she saw watchman walk thru the door...

she took another sip of coffee, and greeted him with a special sort of hug not quite usual for dorothy's standards...

hugs themselves were a bit foreign in general for dorothy's standards, but this time was different...

watchman responded in kind, exalted in actually seeing her there...

little did he know, at this time, that she was there hoping to catch a glance of him...and that she had just evacuated herself of any blockage she may have thought existed in her words...

she got up to get watchman a cup of coffee, when he grabbed her wrist...

turning around, she saw tears in his eyes...

not streams mind you...nor gullywashers or floods,
but a simple moistness that just let her know what
he was about to say...

she saved him the trouble and simply nodded,
saying..."yea...me too..."

...chapter two...

...house of the rising mug...

—

when dorothy got back to the table, she started discussing the reading idea with him, including the fact that she would introduce some of dust's works, as well as some of his own pieces...she even tried to convince him to read his own stuff himself...

he declined gracefully, but was thrilled about dust getting her recognition...and...if dorothy really wanted to read some of his stuff, well, she could do it if she wanted to, but he wasn't the 'public speaking' type...

although she disagreed with that thought, she was at least grateful that he agreed to the readings... and to the luck of seeing him again in the first place...

"i'm really just so glad that i caught up with you today", she said sincerely...

"me too", watchman replied, while he took a sip of some surely awaited brew...

dorothy, noticing his 'enthusiastic thirst', softly asked..."is that your first of the day?..."

watchman, putting down the coffee, while still looking at it, responded,..."yea...and it's real good too..."

"glad you like it...", dorothy said, while quickly changing the mood,..."and you drink it black like god intended..."

that made watchman smile...

he took another sip and then slyly remarked...

"i think that's the first time i ever heard you mention god..."

not to be outdone, dorothy came back with..."hey... when it comes to coffee..."

she raised her cup and shot the rest of it down her throat, following it with a simple..."amen"...

...alternate perking...

—

"we gotta get you a phone...", she blurted out, remembering her thought from earlier...

"...that's a great thought, but...", watchman said hesitantly, "...ya' kinda know i can't afford a phone right now...don't know when i will be able to..."

dorothy assured him that she would take care of it...

he didn't want to accept it at first, but he did accept the fact that, if they were gonna keep in contact, they needed something, and there wasn't a good likely hood that he would have email anytime soon, so, he agreed, and they went to a shop a couple doors down to pick up one of those 'pay-as-you-go' phones...

"alright, now...", dorothy said..."i don't want you to be shy using this, alright...i put a hundred minutes on it, and i can always add more if you need it..."

watchman laughed, thinking that a hundred minutes would be way more than he would ever need...

"can you actually stop and think that a hundred minutes of your life would be wasted taking on the telephone..."

dorothy stopped for a second, really thought about that, and then replied...

"well...you could always text me too..."

watchman thanked her, and she thanked him for accepting it, because she had a feeling he would be using it more than he ever imagined...

...completely jazzed...

—

dorothy and watchman went back to the 'brewed' and she told him that his first call had to be to jazz, to let him know the good news...

watchman hit the buttons slowly, as dorothy read out the number to him...

"we better put that thing on speed dial", dorothy laughed sincerely..."...i'll give you my number too...after you talk to him..."

jazz picked up the phone and a smile came over watchman's face...it was actually the first time he used a cell phone, but more importantly, it was the first time he actually talked to the man who was helping him...helping dust...get her words out there...

jazz was grateful to watchman and promised that he would do his best...he also wanted assurance that watchman would be at the reading, to which, watchman promised...

"he wants to talk to you...", watchman said, as he handed dorothy the phone...

acerbically, dorothy took the phone and immediately yelled, "what???..."

jazz could only continue his thought, disregarding her obvious charm...

"listen..., he said, "...call me later with all the details after you're done, alright?..."

dorothy just responded with a 'yea...yea...can't talk right now, gotta go, bye...', and hung up...

dorothy looked at watchman looking at dorothy... and for a second, they both wondered how they ever got to this point in time...

...still life...
—

watchman took a big swig from his cup, almost like he was trying to build up courage to say something...

dorothy just grinned behind her own mug, wondering what could possibly be on his mind...

with a whisper of a breath, watchman said..."ya' know...", and then he just paused...

dorothy, prodding him along, said..."yea...ya' know what?..."

watchman, taking another sip, put down his cup and continued..."i...i just want to keep this all in focus, ya' know...i mean...i appreciate everything you've done for me, believe me i do, and...i'm sure dust would have appreciated it as well, so i'm not looking a gift horse in the mouth or anything here..."

dorothy smiled, and tried to relieve his anxiety... "well...other than you just calling me a horse, don't worry...i know how you feel..."

watchman, jumping on the tailend of dorothy's sentence, quickly replied..."yea...but i don't want to lose sight of the fact that...this is not about a story, or a book...or words on a page, or readings... this is about a life...one that slipped away from us...and yea, maybe she had herself to blame a little...maybe alot of what happened to her was... well, nobody put a gun to her head, but...she was still a life..."

bringing the table to an almost-complete silence, watchman fiddled with his coffee cup, while dorothy leaned over the table, closer in to watchman...

"i know...i haven't forgotten..., dorothy spoke softly..."but thank you for reminding me anyway..."

she reached out her hand to him, and he held on to hers tightly...

and for awhile, there were no words between them...

...other stuff...

—

in order to break the silence, without losing the reverie of the moment, dorothy spoke up..."so...i read your stuff and really liked it alot..."

watchman just stared at his cup, and in a gentle voice said..."...i'm glad you liked it...it was just a little gift for you...to say thanx..."

dorothy chimed back..."the gift is in your writing...i was very impressed...i told that to jazz as well... and, as i said before, he would really love for you to read your stuff, but...i understand if you don't want to...but, i'm glad that you don't mind if i do...i really want to share your work..."

"that's how i feel about dust's stuff...", watchman said quietly...

dorothy, realizing that watchman was a little out-of-sorts, once again took his hand and said..."don't worry...seriously...she's in good hands...i won't let her get lost between the other stuff..."

watchman smiled a knowing smile, and under his breath responded..."there's always other stuff..."

at that moment, he noticed that his phone was ringing...

he looked at it inquisitively, thinking that, the only person it could be would be jazz, since he hasn't given this number to anybody else...

he held it out towards dorothy, to which she responded..."well, answer it..."

he opened it up to discover that a text message had been sent, by a number other than jazz's...

he pushed the button and began reading it...to himself...

dorothy, curiously inquired..."so...what does it say..."

watchman, sheepishly responded..."it says...'have a nice day'..."

dorothy laughed, and simply followed up with, "...well, if the phone says so, ya' may as well..."

...straight black and fries to match...

—

watchman sat up a little straighter, pulled his chair a little closer, and politely asked…"do you think i could have another cup?…"

dorothy smiled, especially since this was the first time he ever asked for anything…she liked that… "of course…", she replied in a boisterous voice, "… one straight black coming up…"

she got up and, as she was walking to the counter, she turned back and said…"maybe i'll even spring for some black fries as well…"

and when she got back to the table, true to her word, she had several cups of joe and two orders of black fries…

"you didn't have to do this…" watchman said, referring to the fries…

dorothy quickly responded…"hell i did…i wanted them…if you don't want yours, pass them on to me…"

watchman, jokingly, got very protective of his fries all of a sudden...and then began to eat like a man who hadn't in a very long while...

"ya know...", dorothy said apologetically, "...sometimes, i forget..."

watchman just smiled and said..."good..."

they continued to eat when, after settling in a little more, watchman pulled out some pieces of paper from his coat...

"by the way...", he said with a smirk, "...since you mentioned straight black, that reminded me...i did have a couple more pieces with me that i wrote, if you were interested in seeing them..."

"by all means, hand them over...", dorothy replied with a mouth full of fries and pudding...

watchman laughed at the sight of dorothy with her mouth full, but also over his embarrassment of actually suggesting more of his stuff...

she, however, wasn't...she took a sip, grabbed his stuff and began...

...straight black brownstone...

—

pull the chain

release the rain

let it fall

thru the grate

upon the passing train below

and let them know

and let them soak

upon the platform

upon the rails

upon the tin roof

risin' and flyin' by

blinking as they pass

frame by frame

'til the next exit stop

'til they feel every drop

...soaking thirty-nine...

—

beneath the breath

within reach

the atmosphere

of the sphere

the oracle inside

the prophet redeems

the giver receives

the stream flows constant

of thoughts and visions

and deep within

beneath the breath

it lives

...point of return...

—

another loss...and another...

time is a blessing...and an adversary...

too much too young...

smiles extinguished except in our hearts...

there they live forever...

should i but leave a smile in someone's heart

before my loss...

something to be remembered...

something to be held onto...

we all need something

to hold onto...

may i impart the same...

...home with you...

—

well, it was somewhere in a paper...stuck inside one in-between...another headline from a paper... in an old-time magazine, and i said...honey can you read this to me...seems it ain't much makin' sense...she said you got it upside down, turn it around...and mail to this address...
now, she was sittin' all alone, yea, i mean...she was just there all alone, she wasn't...talkin' on the telephone, she was...starin' at the walls, and i just...stared from across the room...with a certain kind of view...and i don't think that she noticed, but i could swear...i felt some chemistry there... and i said...i wanna go home with you, yea, go home with you...
she was dressed in her persuasion, never...looking for a compliment, only...seeking something more in life, that she...never really noticed, and i...noticed there was something about...the way the light shined into her eyes...and it's true, yea, true...i wanna go home with you, yea, home with you...
and i can tell by your smile that you're not waiting for someone...but you've been waiting all your life for someone, and i have to ask you...just to ask yourself...where have you been all my life...
now there ain't no music playin'...but the sound of swayin' in my head, lets me know the trumpet's blastin', all the music that keeps shattering...the

shadows that are constant...in temptation for us
all...and i heed the call, to you...i wanna go home
with you, just to go home with you...
well i reached into the pocket...of my life, but it
was empty...but it isn't that i squandered...all i
had when i had plenty, it's just...the bumpers that
i bounced off of...and the corners that i turned...
they were all my lessons learned, to follow thru...i
wanna go home with you, yea, home with you...
the way you're sittin' aint real pretty...not that you
aren't pretty, it's just that...you just seem so lonely,
while you're...sittin' all alone, and i was...thinkin'
'bout the rest of my life...and how this night could
be the start...of something right, yea, something so
right...
and i'm sending out this invitation...caffeine-laced
to help it reach its destination...don't fear no empty
pockets or the sound of some old bones...that get
in the way...'cause all i have to say to you, is...i
wanna go home with you, yea, go home with you...

...house on fire...
—

there's someone still in there and there's someone
tryin' to get them out, but their house is on fire and
the smoke is startin' to settle in, and
the roof is collapsing tonight from the weight of all
they brought in

there's an orange sky against a blackened night,
and the moon is cryin'
for another soul and another life, 'cause their
house is on fire, and they don't know how to stay
alive, the walls are closing in, but where to begin
to survive

match is struck on a sulfur tip, flame keeps rising
till there's nothing left, frame is shaky and it's
settling in, the doors are gone and the air is thin

there's someone still wanting someone to make it
out in time, 'cause their house is on fire and it's
burning alive

...incesense...
—

dark mahogany lips
hold the incense
and presence

with a wisp of smoke
into the hold
not knowing yet open

surrounded by shade
and depth

so fragile in
its place

yet specific

in purpose a thing of beauty
a gift within

surrounded by shade
and depth

...whisper like a flame...

—

a kaleidoscope upon the water...a ripple abundant...

a breath of winter's presence...and a sun of hopeful spring...

drops of heaven fall...and shine like diamonds with the prism of time...

slowly...specifically...magnificently glistening...

a kaleidoscope upon the water...

a ripple abundant...

...five forty-nine a.m. paradise within...

—

the sun rises on bleecker street

revealing the concrete and all life within...

the air is dewy, and the morning mist is privy

to the aromatic blend brewing within...

the buildings are breathing, as lights begin to flicker

and a host of the incumbents begin to unlock

the treasures within...

the gutter is filled with moon-soaked adulation

as the pavement unravels

all its secrets within...

and i breathe...

deep within...

and the holy spirit fills within

the air i breathe...

as the sun rises on bleecker street...

...life is but a steam...

—

dorothy rubbed her eyes and yawned, giving watchman the impression that she wasn't too impressed...

"everything o k.?", he inquired...

"yea, fine...", she said..."...just tired of how good you are...", she joked...

watchman looked with a bit of a suspicious eye, when dorothy reiterated...

"no...seriously...had a real bad night's sleep...i dreamt that jazz was chasing me all over the city wanting to talk about the book, and then, every time i tried to get on the subway, he was the conductor and he wouldn't start the damn train... oh, it was a nightmare, i tell ya..."

watchman laughed, and confirmed that jazz was actually on their side...

dorothy assured him that he was, and that that was just how they were together...

watchman appreciated the relationship the two of them had...jazz and dorothy...he could tell that they had each other's back whenever and wherever... he also appreciated the relationship that he was building with dorothy...she trusted him when few would...and she had no reason to...

sure, she liked the writings, and was intrigued by dust's story, and, it may have started with that, but...it was becoming more than that...

he looked around and noticed the others in 'the indigo' just minding their own business, doing stuff on their laptops and enjoying their daily cup of joe...and he was amazed at what was going on at his table right there...and how people were so oblivious to it, right under their noses...

as dorothy was about to continue reading, she saw watchman's face and commented..."yea...this whole nation is oblivious lately...thank god for us, right?..."

watchman took one look at dorothy, lowered his head, grinned and said..."yea...thank god..."

...ash backwards...

—

as the place started getting packed, watchman wondered if they should relinquish their table to some other thirsty patrons...

dorothy took a quick scan around, assessed the situation, and simply said, "no"...

she took another sip from her billionth cup, and continued her focused remark with a clearing of her throat, a lit cigarette, and a deep, deep breath...

"i love the fact that you can still smoke in here..."

watchman, looking around, spoke up..."uh...i don't really think you can..."

dorothy, removing the cigarette from between her anxious lips, stared straight at watchman with a look that could have pierced the toughest armor, and proceeded to crush her cigarette out against the wooden table top...

...and with the agility of a dancer, with one hand she picked up her mug, and the other, swatted away the remains of her smoke...

"happy", she said loud enough so that every one in the place could hear her...

watchman, not sure if he should enter this particular cage or not, remained silent for a moment, and then exclaimed..."i guess this is what you meant when you said you were back..."

dorothy took another swig, put her cup down, picked up his papers, and said to herself..."read on macduff..."

...twelve by twelve...

—

thumbing thru the vinyl, the smell of mildew surrounds each intended

awaiting surprise...

each cover to admire...each track listing to remember...

each list of liner notes to inspect...a package wrapped inside a package...

a gift inside a gift...

and what awaits is known, but still a mystery...

and whatever is, whatever comes, is still a surprise...

...drive in turnstile...

—

i am no longer a prisoner

a victim of my own circumstances

as chances should bare

i walked in it blind

the touch of his hem

the touch upon mine

and i walked thru

i walked thru the trail

unraveling the veil

and made it to the place

where i stood face to face

and walked thru

...no longer a prisoner

of this time

...crossing manhattan in a black and white frame of mind...

—

i saw the sun in your eyes as it was going down...i held on tight, hoping
you wouldn't drown...there was still a spark left, and there was still a
tone...there was still a speck of dust, driven to the bone...'cause you were
not alone...

i heard your words so deep, i thought i heard your voice...i saw inside
your soul that night, i had no other choice...i held your hand so tight, it
felt just like a stone...but i knew that life was still inside, right down
there to the bone...'cause you were not alone...

then a shadow passed over, and the streetlight started fading...your head
was still upon my lap, as i continued praying...someone call the sinners
for grief, someone call the saints to atone...someone call the prophet, and
check all his pockets...'cause she ain't goin' home alone...

...refill when necessary...

—

dorothy took a finalizing swig, laid the pages gently on the table in front of her, and asked..."when did you write these?..."

"yesterday...", watchman replied...

dorothy, without skipping a beat, lowered her voice and purred out her feelings..."...son of a..."

watchman, not actually clearly catching dorothy's full remark, asked her to repeat it...

dorothy followed with, "oh, never mind...anyway... it's good stuff...very interesting from a psychotic point of view..."

watchman, looking a bit confused, almost believed her...almost...

dorothy couldn't maintain the facade long enough for him to respond, but simply let him off the hook with a laugh, and a re-appraisal...

"...perhaps from a psychiatrist's point of view...yea, that's it...someone to dig deep into all the layers... ya' got layers kid, did ya' know that..."

watchman just smiled…"yea…but what i don't have is coffee", he said turning over his empty cup…

"oh, coming right up your majesty", dorothy responded, in an all-too playful mode…

watchman continued smiling, as dorothy went to the counter for another fix…as she walked, she even wondered what came over her…she's not usually this 'subservient' to anyone…

…and when she got to the front of the line, she placed her order, which, the new, unfamiliar barista, got completely wrong, not knowing what 'straight black' meant, and just trying to wing it in the process…

dorothy's mind filled with more rust than any coffee cup could carry, and when she got back to the table, immediately started to write…

...darling whirvish...

—

dorothy started writing feverishly, as she grabbed her pad and pen and all but ignored watchman...

watchman knew that look, and he wasn't about to interrupt her at all...

he just sat quietly, sipping his coffee as peacefully as possible, with one eye on dorothy and a peripheral view on the rest of the house...

page after page flew like a cartoon juggernaut from dorothy's pad, and there was no sign of stopping her, not that anyone would dare try...

she was in her own little world, apart from the coffee shop...or the table...or watchman...she was reeling...she was seething...she had bile billowing... and she liked it...

after a brief respite, upon which she blew back, what was now, her drenched hair, she looked up at watchman, who was eagerly looking back at her...

she smiled, and then went back into complete dorothy mode by exclaiming..."what are you looking at?..."

"a familiar face...", watchman stated...

dorothy paused, ignoring any reference to her immediate burst of words, and simply, and calmly, asked watchman..."so...got anything else..."

watchman felt, at this point, he knew dorothy just well enough to turn the table on her, by suggesting that, before he ponies up any more of his stuff, he wanted to hear what she had just coughed up...

dorothy took one look at him, one look at her pages, one look over to the inept barista behind the counter, picked up her pages, shook them once for good measure and said..."let's begin..."

...get it, got it, good...

—

why do we have such short attention spans...

we praise someone one day and vilify them the next...

we demean someone to the point of ridicule and shame, only to forgive them if they happen to release a catchy tune on the radio or finally make a movie we actually wanna see at the box office...

and who are these people who decide who is 'box office'...certainly not the box office...

they force upon us these so-called 'celebrities' that frankly should be working at fast-food chains, if they could even handle that much...

...and apparently, at least, one of them has made his way to a coffeehouse in soho...

...underwhelming overture...

—

don't know why...

they don't even try...

and it's not like they

have to do anything...

...except do nothing...

the holy spirit will do

it all...if they let him...

and that's all they

have to do...

but they don't...

don't know why...

...into the next...

—

how can you smile...after what you've done to the
world...and how can

you laugh...after you trashed everything that's
left...and how can you feel

proud...when the silence has grown loud and the
darkness that

surrounds...has crashed into the next

how can you say...everything's o.k...and how can
you believe...that what

you did was right...and how can you stand...with
your head held high

while the exit where you're bound...is coming up
next...

look back...face tomorrow if you can...

acknowledge or apologize...how can you not be...
you're not

real to me, you never were...i just waited for the
next

...spit-n-vinegar...

—

now don't think me coarse, just 'cause my throat's a little hoarse, and the fact i throw verbal darts at everyone i meet...it's just the way that i am, no excuses, not in this lifetime (...and if you play your cards right, i'll be nice to you...i swear...)

but don't count it...

i mean, ya' never know what's gonna happen, and probably it will be something to tick me off one way or another, and brother, wherever you are bound, don't go looking for no flowers in this garden party, because this is invitation only, and i ain't handing any out lately...i like being alone...i like being by myself...i'm the best company i could give me, plus i get the best answers to all of my questions, so just leave it at that and we'll get along just fine...

but don't count on it...

...dry cough...

—

nothing...

nothing has changed around here...

it never does...

ashes fly

amongst the incinerator

of our lives

yet

there is no fire...

so...

nothing ever changes...

nothing ever does...

...based on a novel approach...

—

"well...i think that's enough for now...", dorothy said confidently...

"oh, i don't know...", watchman said catching his breath, still enveloping dorothy's diatribes..."...i'm sure you have alot more in there just waiting to come out..."

"...i just might...", dorothy countered, as she grabbed her mug with a certain aire...

watchman, smiling, responded..."well...it's nice to know you're not getting soft on us..."

dorothy gulped, as she almost did a spit-take with her coffee...

"you don't know how scary that just was...", she said..."...that was way too much like something jazz would have said...in fact, he did say that to me just the other day..."

"great minds think alike...", watchman commented, as he also took another smirking sip...

"ya know...", she countered..."i'm really looking forward to this reading now...it's gonna be interesting...and it's still not too late if you want to read your own stuff...", dorothy remarked...

"i'll tell ya' what...", watchman interjected..."...i'll think about it...but don't quote me..."

"i wouldn't dream of it...", dorothy said, "...i'm just grateful you're considering it..."

she raised her cup and drank to the possibility... then, she just had to add..."...but i won't quote you on it..."

...chapter three...

...meanwhile...

—

after her afternoon with watchman, dorothy made her way back to her brownstone to put some more thought into her thoughts, and to somehow figure out all the pieces of a very complicated puzzle...

now, it's not to say that dorothy was perplexed... far from it...dorothy was always good at organizing things in her life, especially if she was the one who put them in there in the first place...

but this now was different...

here she was faced with a floor filled with notes, and papers, and stacks, and cards and letters and everything else possible that wouldn't fit on her desk...

"...and this all started because i wanted to write a book", she thought...

one thing she was consoled about was the fact that watchman now had a phone...at least she knew she could contact him when she had more details figured out, which was what she was trying to do now...

she first thought about her book…"o.k…i finished
it and gave it to jazz…he gave it to the publisher…
it hasn't been released yet…"

one down…

"o.k…i gave him dust's stuff, and that too he gave
to his publisher who wants to print it, and that
isn't out yet either…"

step three…

"now…i have watchman's stuff, which, i would love
to get published as well…i have to get copies of
these to jazz…"

next…

"o.k…i have to call jazz and tell him to cancel that
radio gig…i don't have time for that stuff right
now…we have the reading on thursday, which is
tomorrow nite, but that's o.k…it's o.k…i can handle
this…i'm back…remember…"

...seconds in...

—

dorothy kept talking to herself, and to amelia, in the hope that it would help her get her things together...and right now, there were just so many things...

"i could kill jazz...", she said, for no apparent reason other than to blame someone...

and, although life may have seemed a bit complicated at this point, dorothy kinda liked a challenge, whether she would admit it to herself or not...

"alright...", she thought, "...i have to figure out what pieces i'm going to do of my own...that's first... then...i have to figure out what pieces of dust's i'm going to read...then...watchman's stuff..."

o.k...she kinda knew where she was going at this point, trying not to forget her previous points, starting with calling jazz to make sure he didn't set up that radio gig...

she got his voicemail...

"yea jazz...listen...about that jeremiah kent show thing...i just got way too much to do, so let's skip

that for now...but i did have a great time with
watchman, and he will be there tomorrow nite...
whether he'll read or not, i'm not sure...but...oh
yea...and i want to publish his stuff too, so let your
publisher know there's a third book coming...o.k...
i'll talk to you later, call me, o.k..."

...and with that, she was done talking before she
ever heard the beep...

...back at the jazz...

—

on the other side of town, jazz carpenter was starting up his next graphic novel, once again featuring his lead crime fighter, 'crooner'...

"...armed with only a mic stand and a long black coat, crooner roams the

streets at night, taking in every nook and cranny within the heart of his

noir skyline...

he doesn't do it because he believes in justice...he knows there's no such

thing...he doesn't even do it to help out the police... they'll just as soon

arrest him...

no...he does it for all the soaked up souls who don't have anywhere else

to turn, and he knows that in this crazy vagabond world, that's a whole lotta rosie...

what he comes across and who he comes across is anybody's game...but

there's a scrapheap born every minute, and too many bodies laid waste

upon it...and he was tired of it...

"games are for little kids to play...", he thought... "and i'm thru playin'..."

he knew, in his heart, that he wasn't gonna stop all the injustice in

metrock...no screwy squirrel in an overcoat was gonna make a dent in

this copper kettle...he just felt like he needed to be there, and be there he

would be, whether anybody liked it or not... thankfully most of them

did..."

...welcome to metrock...

—

"...got a cold chill this morning, it was dressed as a warning, it was

breaking the door down, with its ever-growing wind...the sky, it was

painful, and the ground, it was rainfilled, and the desert, was the only

one to sing...can't you feel the thunderous attack upon the streets below

and can't you feel the shattered glass that pierces thru the mistletoe and

can't you understand the truth that's clamoring upon the shore and

can't you realize a dream, defines the final score... this nightmare lives

upon a boulevard of broken trenches and realizing all the time, that

these are just more circumstances and all the while, you sit and smile, avoiding all the allegations and terrified that just in time, your hero

arrives to save the day...don't you know your broken wings are never

gonna fly again and don't you see that there are things that make you

want to just pretend and don't you know, the truth when you hear it...

don't you know, that you should be near it...when the time comes, frozen

spirits will be captured one and all and there will be no second call...got

a cold chill this morning, it was time to settle some old scores, it was

tracks that vibrated with a roar, it was your final chance to breathe,

'cause the sky, it was closing, and the gates, were imposing, and the

night was the only light to see...”

...jazzville inclined...

—

jazz smiled, as he re-read the pages he just completed for 'crooner'...

but his smile didn't last too long, as he hovered over the pages from dorothy...

and, adding incensed to injury, he also noticed that he had a message on his phone...several of them actually...all belonging to one name...

"yes dorothy...", he submitted, after she picked up...

"where da' hell have you been?...", she said with her usual flair...

"i was in the middle of writing 'crooner'...anyway, no matter where i've been, what's got your panties in a bunch...", jazz said in kind...

"...the cheaper the better, baby...", she scoffed...

there was a brief pause from both sides of the fence, when finally jazz gave in..."o.k...i give up... whaddya' want?..."

dorothy pulled back from her phone, stared at it in disbelief, and then retorted…"what are you… from outta town or something…didn't i leave you messages explaining everything…didn't you listen to them…why do i waste my breath on you…"

now it was jazz's turn to pull the phone away from his ear…

after about thirty seconds, he got back on…"ya' done yet…"

"when am i ever done…", dorothy responded…

"true…", jazz replied with experience,…"anyway…i did hear what you said, but i was hoping you might elaborate on them…"

"elaborate?…you want 'elaborate"?…", dorothy said with warning…

"never mind…", jazz said, stopping her from going into another brain meltdown…

...dot net...

—

jazz knew it was a losing battle trying to match vicarious wits, or verbal swords, with dorothy...

he just conceded and continued on...

”yes...i’m glad you got to meet up with watchman, i’m glad he’s excited...and yes, i’m glad you got him a phone, that was very nice of you...it was nice talking with him before...and yes, you’ll be ready tomorrow nite and i’ll see you two there...but no, you don’t want to do the radio gig, although i can’t understand why, but nevertheless, it’s o.k...”

dorothy took advantage of jazz’s pause by filling in the blank with...

“now...was that so hard...”

with that ice broken, jazz and dorothy kept on talking for about another thirty minutes, while they actually did straighten out a few things, including wanting to get watchman’s pages published as well...

“well...”, he said...“...i’m not surprised...i don’t suppose you have a title yet for this one, do you?”, he asked, assuming she would...

much to his surprise, she didn't, but, as she said...
"i'm working on it..."

of course, what she was actually working on was figuring out how to talk to watchman about it, without him thinking that dust was being...well, left in the dust, so to speak...

dorothy paused once again, shaking her head... "yea...i'm thinking about it..."

...morning has shattered...

—

after having spent the better part of the evening going thru piece by piece, bit by bit, making sure nothing was forgotten, dorothy woke up grudgingly the following morning, with only one thing on her mind...

...coffee...

no phone, no light, no motorboat could keep her away from her appointment mug, and with that being said, she slipped into a volumous blend of brewed turkish delight...

"the thicker the better", she thought, as she let the lease on her coma expire...

with one eye open, and steam drifting up upon the vapors of an orgasmic nature, dorothy purloined the process of knowledge that today was the day for the book reading, and suddenly tomorrow was looking like a much better world...

she sat her coffee down on her desk, followed immediately by her head, which cradled the mahogany with splendor, as amelia looked on...

there was something about the comfort of the wood that made her think of watchman's discomfort, and, without even the ability to think yet, her eyes popped open with an idea that, to even her thinking, was a good one, because she felt like it wasn't her idea to begin with, like it came out of the ether of the aroma that was begging her to take another sip...

and so, she obliged...

...narrow is the way too often...

—

she stared at her phone...and stared at her phone...

she was amazed that no one had called...no one...

especially not jazz, who by now, would have usually destroyed any semblance of a cohesive morning for her...but no...

and she didn't hear from watchman., but, that she figured, wasn't expected anyway...

she quickly looked at the clock, noticing, not so much what time it was, but how much time she had...

she knew from past experience that time can fly by, especially when you don't want it to, so...

what to do...

she had to go over the pieces she picked for herself...

she had to go over the pieces she picked from dust...

and...she had to go over watchman's stuff, and find out if, perhaps, he would read it or if she would,

and if he would want to read something other than
what she picked...

this was way too much way too early...

she needed another cup...she needed rust...

...pieces of ache...
—

with a fresh cup within her and another on the way, dorothy calmed down, for a moment, and systematically decided to concentrate on her 'set list' for the evening...

of course, she had no clue as to what she was gonna do, despite all her efforts the previous day...

she kept going back and forth, thru pages of stuff that she wrote, and came across a piece called 'ticonderoga'...she had remembered she liked it when she wrote it, so she re-read it just to be sure...

"...words are just shavings from the point of a pencil...the center led lifted to exact the point unto which the message is spoken...but the ashes of shavings display the message revealed..."

'o.k.', she thought, 'but...that kinda reminds me of something else i wrote...'

thumbing thru the pages, she discovered one called 'number two pencil'...

'the titles are even similar', she said to amelia, who was in her frame close by...dorothy began to read this one, but indeed with less enthusiasm...

"number two pencil, left alone on the desktop, wants to unravel, but it knows that it cannot... take off the yellow, that is trapping the ashes, roll around on your hightop now, to reach the ever after...and it would, if it could, split the wood, split the wood, as it dares to share, the graphite that it bled, just trying to get to the led..."

'well', she thought, '...they are similar...but at least this one rhymed...'

she sat back forcefully, looked up to the ceiling and screamed...'my god...now i'm justifying them by whether they rhyme or not...'

at this point, she was about to pack it in...but she had some hope when she came across her next piece...

...and the band plays on...

—

the shimmer of purple light

passes as the notes upon

the lines of

sheet music...

the sun shines

upon the body

of the bass

as the fingered display

gently cascades fluidity

upon the strings...

and the band plays on...

...prosed and conned...

—

between the coffee stains and the crinkles in the paper, she actually like that one, despite the fact that it was all too clear that she was starting to not like anything she herself wrote...

'i think maybe dust wrote this one...or perhaps watchman...', she jestered, knowing full well that, it was, indeed, her own creation...

but it was also clear to her that the two of them had been having a great influence on her, both professionally and personally...

then again...it was this realization that also led her to the conclusion that, after reading dust's stuff and watchman's pieces, her words of wisdom and witlessness had little importance...

...although...the last piece did give her hope...

'now...if i could only find more like that one', she thought to herself, as she scrambled thru her prose...and cons...

she laughed, thinking that would be a good name for the evening's festivities...'...prose and cons...'...

maybe she would even change the name of her book before it went to press...maybe not...

but anyway...with fingers crossed, cup brimming with rust-filled goodness, and a wink to old amelia, dorothy moved on thru her bits and pieces, gazing intently for something that even resembled what she was looking for...

a little while passed, as well as a few more shots of java confidence, but she finally stumbled upon an interesting piece, that, well...at least it looked interesting...but she had to read it again, just to make sure...

...nothing else...

—

there were moments when i left you
moments that i lost you
moments when i hurt you
even double-crossed you
but moments that were tender
gentle and serene
were all i ever wanted
why did i have to be me

i'm no good...i'm wrong
i don't have the strength to carry on...

i'm just bad...bad for you
i'd lie just to tell you the truth
'cause there's nothing else i know how to do

there were times when we were happy
times when things seemed right
times when i would hold you
in the middle of the night
but there were times when i went missing
and i wasn't there for you
and where i was, was where i wasn't
being true

i'm no good...i'm wrong
there's no reason for you to carry on...

i'm just bad...bad for you
i'd cry just to find my way thru
then i'd wipe away the doubt that i knew
'cause there's nothing else i know how to do...

...coffee on the half-shell...

—

dorothy sat there, humming the tune over and over again...

it was actually a song she wrote many years ago for a relationship that, in her mind, should have never been...

'...but it's still a damn good tune...', she thought to herself, as she continued singing it out loud at the top of her lungs...

it was moments like this that she was thankful she lived in a brownstone, with only an attic above her and enough space below not to disturb anyone...

she really loved her apartment, as small and mildew infested as it may have been...

'oh, the stuff i have written here', she thought, as the years kept flooding back into her brain...

and as she continued thinking, it wasn't long before her confidence began to rise again...

'after all...', she surmised...'i did write a few good things over that time...maybe those were so good because i wasn't trying to write them, i had no intent behind them...'

she glanced over at a pile of pages that were some of her more recent efforts, and she actually gave a little sneer to them...

she went into her bedroom and pulled out several heavy boxes, and started ripping into them like she was ripping into some idiot that would annoy her...

'now if i could just find...', she began thinking, as she rummaged the lot...

she didn't really know anything specific she was looking for...she just figured she would know it when she found it...

...and this was one of them...

...tired of the night...

—

draw the shades, turn off the tv
and dim the lights way down low
light up another cigarette, and all I see
is the smoke rising from the glow

and I'm so tired of the night
the minutes pass like hours waiting for the morning
light
so tired of another lonely night
waiting for you in the shadows of light

like a fool, I keep deceiving
myself, into leaving it all behind
but if I keep on believing, that while I'm awake I'm
dreaming
I'll only go out of my mind

'cause I'm so tired of the night
the minutes pass like hours waiting for that
morning light
so tired, of another lonely night

waiting for you...I'm waiting for you

as the candle slowly burns, I got no place left to turn
and the flame that once burned bright, just won't
see me thru the night...

'cause I'm so tired of the night

...between a rock...

—

surprisingly for dorothy, as she rumbled thru her 'leftovers', as she would call them, she realized how many songs that she wrote dealt with heartbreak, or just simply breaking up...

'i never had my heart broken'...she thought to herself with a grin, '...but i sure broke alot of hearts...', she had to continue on with...

she also came to a clear realization that, she was never really good with relationships in general...

not a whole lot of friends, not a whole lot of lovers... never really cared to have too much of either...

'it's never good to have too much of anything...', she exclaimed,...'that's why cookie companies doesn't make a 'triple-stuff'...'

she started laughing at that, for no real reason, because, even she realized it wasn't that funny...

but at this point, exhaustion and pressure was getting the best of her, in a very peculiar way...

no more was she interested in the book she wrote, or at least, what was in it...now she was concentrating on that record album she always wanted to put out...and possibly how this nite could rectify that situation...

now, she knew she wasn't gonna be doing some karaoke while she was up there, but she quite possibly would throw in some of her old lyrics... just for fun...

...after all, rock stars do have way more fun than authors anyway...

...and a harder place...

—

she kept going thru her song sheets, as well as pots of coffee that would rival columbia's best drinkers...

she was also causing a major cloud formation over the middle of manhattan, with more smokes than a bookie joint...

but she didn't care...

she started feeling a fire that had been missing for a long time now...and though she was still 'dorothy', she was a more complete 'dorothy' again...with all the baggage, all the brine, and all the balls...

and, as she ripped thru a couple-a-dozen sheets of songs, she stumbled on one that was a real rocker...one she always would tear into whenever she was mad...

...and she tore into it alot...

and, although her 'anger' had been honed a bit since days gone by, it still didn't detract her from letting loose with this, as she put it, 'classic' track...

...straight down the middle...

—

trapped like a rat and i'm hiding in the corner
getting so hot, it feels like a sauna
can't stand standing in the middle of fear
gotta get out of here...

cast into something i don't wanna get into
feels like there's trouble always waitin' to screw you
ain't no denying' that i'm losing my soul
gotta get back control

and i'll take it...any way i can
straight down the middle...if you know who i am
callin' the shots...all along the way
doncha' come back again...

comin' out fightin' when the bell is rung
hittin' like the hammer of a loaded gun
aimin' at the target with both barrel's loaded
just gotta get goin'...

and i'll take it...i'll take it again
straight down the middle...right around the bend
callin' all the shots...so ya' better listen
'cause soon i'll missin'...

i'm gone...

...still on holiday...

—

totally exhausted, fully drenched, dorothy was smiling bigger than she had in a long while...

'that...was good...', she thought to herself, as she collapsed in her chair...

"whadidya' think?...", she asked amelia..."pretty cool huh?...i don't think you ever heard that one... man...it's been a long time for myself as well..."

she knew that she wasn't the same person that wrote that so many years ago...but there was still that part of her she missed...and it was refreshing for her to get it back...

she pushed the button on her cd player, and leaned her head back as Billie Holiday gently wisped out of the speakers...

quite a different approach from what she herself was just singing, but there was that dichotomy that lay within her, and the problem she was having all along about this evening...

thinking about this evening, she quickly jumped up, remembering she had to contact watchman...

she dialed his phone, but no answer…she tried texting him as well, but she thought that might just have confused him even more…she never got around to showing him how to text anyone…

she closed her phone and, putting on her robe, ran down the stairs to talk with her landlady, having just been reminded of her 'brilliant idea' from earlier…

…and when she got back up to her apartment, Billie was still beautifully melancholy…

...spice of write...

—

dorothy certainly had her melancholy side...and loved every minute of it...

she would soak in it like some people would soak in a nice warm bath...

but suds and bubbles never really appealed to dorothy, and there were so many sides to wash away, she wouldn't even know where to begin...

one of the reasons, she pondered, why she never followed thru on her 'musical' delivery, was simply because she liked so many different styles of music...

...and this eclectic rendering of her desires and mobility could be seen as a direct link to her inability...apathy need not apply...

but...it didn't stop her from writing some great lyrics, at least she thought so...

and, in hindsight, she realized that some of them were definitely 'signs of the times' and perhaps a little of what the 'signs of her mind' were like at those times as well...

she ran thru a dozen or more pages that clearly were fringe-jacketed moments of peace and love, which she still appreciated...a couple of torchers that would do any vamp proud...and, of course, ones that, let's just say, were simply written down because she felt like writing...

'i gotta put this pile aside', she mused, wanting to give herself, and the songs, the much required dissecting they deserved...

and on the top of this pile was one she originally titled, "...comet vomit...", but was later crossed out and changed to..."...meteor tango..."

...meteor tango...

—

peanuts by the wayside
underneath the floor
make your way past doris day
who's hangin' on the door
and all the little bits you see
are floating so illogically
that you can't understand, until you transgress
and dispose of all your dreams

and you cry out to be heard just one more time
but the images you seek, are simply
poetries of rhyme
and the crimes that you are held for
aren't yours to call your own
and the parasites who listen are just
missing the whole show
they'll have to go...

flashlight in your face
shuffle down the aisle
looking at both ways, until you
cross that extra mile
and then the paperboy, he flings the close
of yesterday's affairs
right next to your front door, he saw you
in your underwear

and you run back to be hidden
one more time again alone
the images are frozen in the mind
so let it go
and the time that you hold back is just a
lack of empathy
the corridors are closed, so now it's
time for you to breathe
but they'll have to leave...

...onions and other strangers...

—

dorothy sat there and read it twice...

not because she thought it was so great or anything, but because she found there was '...something hypnotic about it...'...

when she read it the first time, she saw something in it, but then, when she read it again, she got different meanings out of it, which, in her mind, was like a 'shapeshifter kinda thing' that she had never experienced, or at least, ever realized, before in her writing...and dorothy just thought that it was so cool...

'...bet my new stuff doesn't have any of that cool shapeshiftin' stuff...', she pondered with an aire of certainty...

'what da ya' think amelia...", she asked talking to the photo..."...ya' think any of my new stuff is like this..."...

the photo of miss earhart just sat there on her desk, not replying in the slightest, and yet, dorothy clearly knew she heard her response, to which dorothy replied..."yea...me too..."

she continued staring at the lyrics, hoping they would suddenly peel away in layers, like an onion or something…

dorothy loves onions…and she'll eat them every chance she gets, regardless of her breath…

"ya' like onions amelia?…", she asked the photo once again…and once again, there came no reply, but it did allow dorothy to realize that her focus needed to be, a bit more focused, since her time left clearly was not allowing her to be anything else…

'…how sad…', she thought, as she collected the papers together…

...as time would have it...

—

dorothy, a bit more focused now, tried contacting watchman again, but to no avail...apparently, he really wasn't used to listening for his phone and dorothy could certainly understand that... but still...she did have to contact him as best as possible, as soon as possible...

having been caught up with going thru works and triple thinking her decisions, the hands of the clock slipped around like a rip in the time space continuum...and in the midst of this quagmire, her phone started ringing thru her ears like a icicle shot out of a cannon...

she reached for it like a jackrabbit, making sure that, whoever was on the other end would stay there..."yes...hello...", she shouted into the phone, as a timid voice responded...

"yes...hello?...", said the voice on the other end, which turned out to belong to watchman...

"oh thank god...", dorothy said, allowing the world to slip off her shoulder a bit...

"yes...thank god indeed...", watchman responded,... "it looked like you called me...", he questioned...

"yes, i did", she said, shaking her head..."oh...anyway...i wanted to touch base with you about tonight, which isn't too far off now...are you still coming?..."

"absolutely", he replied...

"...i picked some of your pieces to read...i don't know if you had any in mind...", dorothy inquired...

"i'm sure whatever you picked is fine...", he responded sincerely...

"...and...", she began to ask, "...are you gonna read them?..."

watchman took a beat, and simply said..."no...this isn't about me...not for me anyway..."

...and on the seventh hour...

—

dorothy understood...a bit disappointed...but understood...she had to...time was now creeping into that forbidden zone, that place where she couldn't hold it back, but it just had to go a little slower...

"what am i supposed to be wearing?...", watchman asked cautiously...

dorothy knew that what he had on was pretty much all he had...she put him at ease by simply stating..."what ya' got on is fine..."

and, although she couldn't actually see it, dorothy could hear the smile of relief come over watchman's face...

this made her feel so good...

"so...", she added..."i'll see you there tonight?..."

"yea...i'll be there", he confirmed...

"great...see you in, wow, only a couple of hours... excited?...", she asked...

watchman paused and then, with honesty, made a gesture by saying, "i know you'll be great..."

dorothy, not knowing how to respond, just said "thanx"...and wished him well...

when they hung up, dorothy was even more perplexed than when she started the day, so she made another run for the coffee pot, poured down as much as she could, as quickly as she could, then simply collapsed inside herself on her kitchen floor...

exhausted, but smiling, she rested...

...whole lotta somethin'...

—

practically showtime at 'whole lotta books', and jazz was still 'patiently' waiting for a familiar face to arrive...in fact, any face would do...

there was no dorothy, no watchman, no audience for that matter, so maybe the first two not being there didn't matter much either...but still...he knew that they were gonna start soon, and he didn't have anything to vamp with, so stretching seemed to be out of the question...

the manager came over to wish him well, and to encourage him that 'audiences usually turn out late to these gatherings...unless we have stephen king, that is...'

jazz could have taken that the wrong way, but, since he knew that dorothy never considered herself to be a 'stephen king', he just let it slide...

and at that moment, he noticed dorothy sliding in, calm as ever, which of course jazz took for her being scared or annoyed...

"what's wrong...", jazz asked...

"nice greeting...nothing why...", dorothy replied...

"ya' look good...", jazz mentioned...

"well, thanx, i guess...", dorothy responded curiously..."anyway, we all set here..."

"all but your boy watchguy...", jazz said softly...

"watchman...and what have you got against him, i thought you liked him...", dorothy asked...

"i do...i just wish he was here already...", jazz explained...

dorothy looked at the sweat pouring off his forehead..."what's wrong with you...are you nervous about something..."

"no...not really i guess..."...and with those words, jazz dropped to the floor...

...burning stuff...

—

dorothy rushed to pick him up...her hand touched his forehead and he was burning up...

"are you sick man...you're burning up...", dorothy said briskly...

jazz, coming to, replied, "...overall...i have felt better..."

"let's get you home...i'll call a cab...", dorothy said taking charge...

"what about the gig?...", jazz asked...

"i can take care of it all...", dorothy remarked...

"you couldn't take care of hamster...", jazz said in his declined state...

dorothy let go of him, releasing him back to the floor..."for that remark i should kick you as well... but...listen...i know your concerned...do you trust me?..."

"of course i do, you know that...", jazz sincerely replied...

"then let me do what i have to do, and you do what you have to do...look, watchman's here...everything's alright...", dorothy said with a confident smile...

jazz took one look, said 'thanx', and then made a run out the door in order not to relieve his lunch upon the bookstore carpet...

dorothy laughed and gave watchman a hug... she was truly glad to see him, and tried to make everything seem right on schedule...

as she turned and grinned at the audience starting to make their way towards the seats, dorothy turned to watchman, let her grin slip, and under her breath said...

"...just act like these people are normal..."

...one time seriously...

—

fortunately for dorothy, watchman did seem pretty calm about everything going on...much more than she was...

not that she couldn't do the reading...she wasn't concerned about that...she just didn't want to have to talk to anyone afterwards...she was afraid she might have to hurt somebody...

and as the manager got up to introduce dorothy, watchman tugged at her sleeve and leaned over, whispering..."if you really want me to read, i'll read..."

dorothy lit up like a pack of smokes on christmas day, and she was sure to take advantage of it...

and just as she was about to thank him, the manager called her up to the mic...

dorothy walked over with to the podium, slow and steady...

"thank you...thank you for coming out tonite... here...at, uh...whole lotta books'...i am very grateful that we were able to fill in for the author thomas blake at the last minute...and i hope you enjoy your evening..."

the audience applauded, as dorothy looked, on one hand gratified, and on the other hand, ready to tell them all how ignorant the world was, including all of them...

thankfully, she just opted for the first choice...

...lose your shoes...

—

watchman was amused, noticing dorothy's lip-biting...but as she opened her mouth again, it was more like tongue-biting...

"thank you...you are all very kind...well...just to give you a brief idea of this evening, there will be pieces from three different books read tonite...one of these books, coming soon, will be from our other author present tonite, 'watchman', as well as some pieces from my own book, and, as your wonderful m.c. here mentioned, my name is dorothy rocker..."

once again, applause was forthcoming from a very generous audience...

"now...", she continued..."you may have noticed i said three books, and that's because the third author we are spotlighting tonite is a lady named dust, who cannot be with us tonite...but she will clearly be here in her words..."

the audience, once again, clapped...

"you don't have to clap at everything, ya' know...", dorothy said abruptly...

then, regaining her composure, she offered up…
"but you can if you want…", to which the audience
this time laughed…

"well…", she continued…"once again, i thank you
for coming…we will begin…"

...chapter four...

...crazy on you...

—

dorothy rambled on, as the audience sat politely listening to many pieces that she had included in her book, as well as more than a few that she newly re-discovered as she was plundering her past earlier that day...

it seemed like she had more fun with those, along with her explanation of who jazz was and why he wasn't with them, relinquishing her continued barbs with a final..."he's gonna kill me if he ever finds out, so don't tell him i told you..."...

she shuffled a few more pages, knowing that she soon wanted to introduce watchman up there, before he had time to change his mind...

"i hope you all are enjoying yourselves", dorothy asked, to which smiles and a few claps returned in kind...

"good...", she continued, "...'cause we got alot more stuff for you tonite, and, in fact, i'm gonna start wrapping up my stuff here in a minute so that i can bring watchman on..."

she looked over to the side to make sure he was still there, and, when catching his eye, gave him a smile...

"...and also so i can go have a smoke...", she added, to which the generous audience laughed...

"you are too kind...", she said..."no, really", she meant...

she continued looking thru her pages until she came upon one titled "cricket match", which was paper-clipped with a few others...

"oh, o.k...these are pretty cool...", she said outloud, evoking another laugh, and then, when all got silent again, she began to read...

...cricket match...

—

the crickets are dancing in my head again

as i lay upon my bed again, grasping for the breath
i used to call my

own...

i know i used to, therefore i know i know how to...
but why to...

that seems to be the question for which there is no
suggestion...

and this ringtone that is pouncing, surely doesn't
cure an ounce of

prevention when patience is a luxury that is ill-
afforded, yet accorded...

but the ringing, of course, which i haven't aborted
that lay inside my

skull from dusk till dawn did, only stands to dull
any conscious stream

that may tend to appear once an idea is near...

but never fear...

for the monsters underneath my bed, will scare them off, and make me

cough instead...

as i lay upon my bed again...

with crickets in my head again...

praying that, instead again

they pay rent or they leave...

...hamstring rhapsody...

—

broken edification of a simple explanation
and the righteous indignation of a
prestidigitation
and the power of the struggle
for the last chance of a mug that you can
grab between both hands and cuddle
lying in the middle of the mud
and in your own blood and the
temperature keeps dropping
and there's just no kind of stopping when the
automat reaction is a
self-inflicted traction
and the
sooner is the later
when you see the alley gator climbing
up down from the sewer with a
cup of warm sumatra
and the
tone and simple reflex is the
one that suits you the best
at the moment you're distracted by the
coroners reaction and the
chances for a reason
are too blurred by all the seasons
and the
go betweens are subtle
for the chance of your survival

while the pressure keeps on building and the
war machine keeps killing and the
press is in the papers and the
minds aren't liberated for the
truth that's an injunction for the
heavy set reduction of the
prestidigitation
and the righteous indignation of a
simple explanation
of the broken edification

...neither one way nor the other...

—

face in the typewriter
ghost in the machine
sticking with keys that keep sticking
pressing on for a press release

labyrinth in the spirit
mindset in a maze
thoughts within the fingers touch
memories in a haze

looking at the short end
staring at the long
both sides feeling so divided
but neither one is wrong...

for at the end of every sentence
there is...a pause...

...overfated...

—

i read an all true story, 'bout some innocence and glory, and i hoped that one day better, i would, understand this quarry, and soon i had to realize, my fate was sealed before this day began...

> and i swore unto my conscience that today was
> gonna
> start again

and i told a deadly tale about some woman in a shoeshop where she broke alot of hearts and i was one of them i know, because i asked about her carefully, and i felt my fate was sealed...

> and i swore unto my heart that parts of it were
> gonna heal

at the tender age of zero, i set out to be a hero, but my latter days and all this rain just equaled to be near old, and i started thinking once again, my fate was sealed 'bout thoughts i once had then...

> and i swore unto the letter i was writing that i'd
> find
> another pen

and i broke into a jukebox, it turned out to be a
sandbox, and i asked about my piggy bank, that
was all messed up with congress, and i had a
reputation that i lived up to although my fate was
sealed...

    and i swore unto my spirit that my soul would
always know that it
was real

...crash test mummies...

—

night becomes you, as moonlight falls upon the precipice of your soul

and all the while, circumference fills your mind with extra-narrational notions that you may cheat on your principals

strange surroundings compromise the undergrounding of life's imperfections

and all the while, a change of direction is suited to be the nobler of all causes and causeways

for at the end of the day, life is a pity in this here city, when trembling abounds in the gates marred by hounds

and black is the ruin of everyone's soul, but spice up the joe with a blend from head to toe, of rumors and inconsequences that pertain to literally no one...

no one...

chances are you're right...

...smirk...

—

the king is dead

though the king still lives

he is not a king

he is a fraud

though he sits in his oval chair

he is not there

not by right

but by wrong

so wipe that smirk off your face

the king is dead

...calm of the tepid appetizer...

—

the audience sat still, some amused, some still thinking, 'cause dorothy's 'eclectic' variety certainly didn't give them a clear path to hold on to...

...but that suited dorothy just fine...

"alright...", she piped up, "...one more and you suffer no more..."...and then she added..."...by the way...that last one was written a few years back...", as if to offer up and excuse or something...

she felt she needed to stress that as she zipped thru her pages like she knew there was just one last special one she wanted to end with...

...and when she came upon it, she just knew...

"alright...", she repeated..."this is one i'll end my segment with here..."

she paused to see if anyone would applaud or cheer...no one did...

"thank you for that...", she said under her breath... "anyway...i want to dedicate this one to my two other authors featured here tonite, watchman and dust...this piece is called..."

looking down at her paper, she realized that she never gave it a title, so, just making one up on the spot, she said…"uh…this piece is called…'needle in panic park'…

she waited for a reaction, while in her mind she thought that…

'…well…it wasn't the best choice i could have made…but, i do like the movie "panic in needle park", and i just saw it the other day, so a play on the title is better than saying nothing at all…'

and with that self-convincing righteous indignation under her belt, she faced her awaiting subjects and began…

...needle in panic park...

—

burning thru the atmosphere

the fireball continues on

not raging not misbehaving

but ever constant ever flaming

it can touch it can singe

it can burn from within and light up the night

with its orange and white

this spherical means

of no in-betweens

these flames that reach

and find their paths

thru the atmospheres and hemispheres that once

clogged our minds

to cure the blind

upon the black it moves

upon the sight it delivers

fixing a stare beyond comprehension

ever changing direction yet

knowing quite clear

its intention

...watch and learn...

—

with that finished, dorothy thought the title wasn't so bad after all, yet, nevertheless, wasn't about to stick around to find out what 'they' thought, so...

"without further ado, i'd now like to bring up our other present author for the evening...ladies and gentlemen, watchman..."

she realized, for a second there, she felt like she was introducing led zeppelin at madison square garden, but few took notice, as she was eagerly awaiting to dash off and have a smoke, along with calling jazz to see how he was doing...

but first, she had to stick around to see how watchman would do...

he bent over the mic, a little nervous and somewhat 'out-of-sorts', but, in only a moment, he seemed relaxed and focused on what he was doing, and certainly, what his purpose was for doing it...

"thank you...", he began, as the crowd seemed suspicious...

"...uh...anyway...", he continued..."i will very briefly begin by telling you a little about myself...", he paused to gain some confidence...”...i...have been living on the streets now for some odd time, and...well, how i got there is really of little consequence, but...one thing i discovered during this season that i currently continue to find myself in, and that's how people truly are...and it's not just one simple blanket statement that people like to box themselves and each other in...it's so much more than that...people...people can be so incredible...they have such abilities within them...to do...good things for others...to do for themselves...to get thru whatever they need to...”,...he briefly paused and took a sip of water...”but...”, he continued...”they also have the ability to hurt, physical and spiritually...they can say words that can scar just as easily as a knife...and they can limit themselves and others just by circumstance...”...changing the subject...”i have a friend...had a friend...i really didn't even know her very well until it was too late...you'll get to know her tonite...her name was dust...i'll...i'll read you a few of my bits and then we'll concentrate on her, because it was her life...and the loss of it, that started this one tonite...”

and with that, he never spoke again, except to say the title of his pieces...

...torch...

—

the match is lit...

as the sulfur consumes the tip...

the flame reaches the pen...

bleeding into the ink...

from within its orange hive...

the yellow surrounds...

the red endures...

i've seen this before...

in a different light...

...hot mug in the summertime...

—

this heat...

this very essence of my being...

this element on which i wrap my eternal focus...

this moment that i walk thru with ease...

this breath on which my words linger...

this subtle charm of constancy...

this very essence of my being...

this heat...

...taking applications...

—

when the sticks hit the skins

there is certainty

but when the pedal hits the drum

there is encounter

when the cymbal crashes

there is spark

but when the cymbal is caressed

there is shiver

when voices come together

there is hue

but when one voice matters

there is grey

...ridin' with the bass...

—

fingers

up and down

the frets

smiles

within

each note

scaling

the soul

with blessed company

touching...

with voice...

connecting...

with heart...

ridin'...

with the bass...

...nickles three...

—

the water is still glistening

but the flame still cinders within

and the son

and

nephew play along

as the song reaches the

level

below the above

within the gap

that places it where

it places me

...freeze frame...

—

walking along bleecker street
you make your way up to bowery
dying for a coffee in your hands
you concentrate on the concrete below your feet
and you shuffle as you go
and make your way that much closer
just to understand

and you know once you get there, you'll have to
take some time
to pull your pen and paper, and come up with silly
rhymes
but there's gonna be a moment when the moment
has to bend
and then you're looking at your life
thru a different kind of air
it's a comedy of errors
but no one's laughing in the end

and then you freeze...

staring out on bowery
holding on to coffee
just trying to remember how to breathe
you focus on the notion that if you understand the plan
that somehow you'll envision
your life...starting over again

but you know once you get there, it all will look the
same
the coffee black won't take you back, to where you
already came
and that moment when it hits you, and you just
have no strength
to hit it back
you find yourself looking at your life
thru a vacant hologram
a star-filled aberration
but no one wants your autograph

and then you freeze...

staring out on bowery
holding on to your coffee
just trying to remember how to breathe...

...audio visceral...

—

naked ice drips fire from my arid veins as
corpuscles sweat their way

thru a myriad of crossbound tentacles that
manage to engage all the

impulses that expose...

with eyes of cymbaline, this centipede of
questioning still stands to

envelop the relative set-up that once commanded
a presence now

simply undressing...

and the skin's gravity shows maladies that have
yet to make themselves

known to those surrounding a pleasant
abounding, but chancing the

elements to ravage the cellophane condition that
tradition suffocates...

and dawn nearly breaking only enhances my
inhibitions to such a

fruition of scaling back the layers of membrane
that try to escape

between the visionary and topiary paths
exchanged...

and in the market place, the race continues to
review the last of the

individuals who mark their territory with stories
that embellish the

legendary and plagiarize the soul alone...

...tunelighting...

—

thru comprehension and tension strolls
the climbing of the rock and bitter rolls
   the horses down the avenue
are selling bread and bargaining shoes
      between the right and alleyways
      and cause descent for better days
      the sun can grip an iron moon
      and let loose with its own sweet tune
   within the bars that lock behind
the doors that swing in quarter time
   the blessing of the gone again
the trampled hope of once was when
      and echoes subtle, milked by double
      are quarreled apartments for rented struggle
      and cages lie down by dirty old thrones
      of sentiment and sorrow's tone
for bastions that bow forever between
   their understanding for the queen
thru visions and shackles and waistcoats on high
   deliver the goods with no single reply
      the message is sent, but somehow where it went
      is beknownst by the messenger, who now is dead
      so cold winds and minstrels and songs from the shire
      are tempered with riddles that truth must acquire
the dimples at last are the temperatures brew
   for horses escaping down the avenue

...in the road...

—

old man in the mirror
where ya' runnin' to

old man in a body
that belies your youth

old man with a new plan
dontcha' know the truth

old man won't you listen
can't ya' hear the proof

salad days, drift away
on a blanket of night air
to reveal all the currents
dragging yesterday's news somewhere

old man in the puddle
why don't ya' get off your shoes

old man in the middle
tryin' to chase away yer blues

old man in the scuffle
ya' only fight to lose

old man what's the trouble
what ever happened to you

...ashen veil...

—

another grey day in my sight
when i awake and know that something just ain't right
the sun is up but barely in my view
and i can't see, any colors, in the frozen hue

but the fire is still burning
and the dreams never went to sleep
'cause the world keeps on turning
but it's still, at the edge, of my feet...

another street...they all look the same
but i tell you the truth...i don't know who's to blame
the shadow's gone...but darkness still increases
over heavy raindrops falling, over life, between the
creases

and the fire...still entices
while the ember gives a glow...like a streetlight shinin'
and the dishes that are filled...with the thoughts of
all who's will
is stronger still, at the edge, of my feet

another sunrise...to chase the moon away
so whisper softly...till you cannot breathe today
dedicate...this site unto the morning
and rest amongst the best, there is to be, inside
this warning

'cause the fire…wants your patience
as the bodies…crave more engagements
contact present and alive…for those who have not died
but still i find, at the edge, of my feet…

...touch the coal...

—

catch up with the train that has already departed
the stationary rail
from which you started...

feel the short

sharp

shocks

of electrical fire within the wheels
that turn and yearn for that next
track of wax
to engage upon...

find that groove
and catch up
with that train...

...groundwave...

—

hear the siren song they sing
the freedom of the bell that rings
the temple of the frozen light
the rocks so high at night they climb

the moon so hot it burns like fire
the wind so cold it warms your feet
you touch the rocks with great awareness
you shroud yourself in only heat

your hair is raised beyond suspicion
your eyes are focused on the view
the only grass you see is lifted
betwen the stones you ever knew

and the hope that keeps them going
and the fixed epitaph
that belies only ruins
and the tunes still left within

see the pavement start to shuffle
see the faces all in line
thru a glass that's like a prism
destorting only space and time

walking past they never notice
the noticer who always sees
the random of the troubled warrior
the constant of the one who dreams

and the peace that keeps on showing
thru the souls eternity
beneath the streets of knowing
and the beats still left beneath

...incident report...

—

ashes from the flame that suits you all around

recognizing the fire's presence

feeling the singe upon the weight of the world

and holding into submission

pressed within the flesh and

trampled underground

ashes from the flame

that suits you all around

...mondo grey...

—

sweat pours off
like a central nervous system
waiting to explode...
traffic seems to congest
as the noise
reaches it's
optimum level...
swirling in
my head, my focus
has waves running
across its view...
...and all the
while, the soundtrack gets
louder and louder...
all alone, yet
so many...the aroma is
stale...
the boxes are
lined up like a supermarket
check-out...
'no sale...no sale' keeps
ringing up the
soul to the wasteland...
cut-off,
selected, from the
rushing passing by...
and the noise is congested,

blocking
pathways to the sky...
no reaching out, no reaching in...
tempted, curious...but
time has
stopped here...

...single vocal theory...

—

there is only one voice necessary to express one soul...

there is only one soul necessary to display one spirit...

multiple voices from multiple rooms

causing conspiracy to confuse the issue...

and still

there is only one soul to listen...

...taste is sweeter...

—

only a dream...that's what it seemed...
thinking 'bout, how time has flown
beyond its broken seams...

sunrise ahead...sunset behind...
staring at the darkness, that has
occupied your mind...

breathing in...breathing out...
just another thing, that you don't
really think about...

looking up...looking down...
not sure, if your next door
will see you swim or drown...

but you swallow down the bitter pill
that you must finally take
the corridors of hell are waiting
for your next mistake
the tolling bell keeps yelling out
adventures of mistrust
while you are left there waiting
your life is skating on the rust

only a life...that's what they say...
one step here, the next step
somehow gone away...

breathing out...no longer breathing in...
one too many times, you tried
but tired always wins...

and you understand why both your hands
must grab the mug again
to drink the nectar of the gods
that somehow lies within
the steeplechase cannot erase
the saber's mighty thrust
when shivers fill your quiver...and you're left with
only dust

...shoreline for all those no longer drowning...

—

as watchman finished reading his final piece, dorothy noticed his eyes...

as deep as they had always seemed, now they were distracted by something obvious...

as the receptive audience waned down to silent hum, dorothy realized there was no going on for watchman anymore, and she quickly went to his side and held him, for what, to watchman, seemed like forever...

"how 'bout a nice hand for watchman, ladies and gentlemen...", dorothy proposed, as the crowd once again showed their appreciation...

watchman showed little of his, as he was still frozen in a moment other than this one...

in his mind, he was back in that alley, with that head on his lap, and his friend kane by his side...

he felt a loss now far greater than just these two souls...his whole world has gone from somewhere out there, to somewhere in here...and he wasn't sure exactly which was the correct one...

dorothy continued to distract the crowd, while she started talking about dust, and the pieces that she would be reading next...

watchman jerked for a moment, and then came back to the mic, only to remind the listeners about "...the preciousness of, not just life itself, but the life within the self..."

he slumped his shoulders and walked aside, as the crowd hushed in reckoning...

dorothy, holding back some tears herself, carried on, by announcing to the crowd that she would start reading, what would essentially be, the 'dust' portion of the evening...

...chapter five...

...d string...

—

watchman sat down to catch his breath...

dorothy looked over to make sure he was gonna make it through the rest of the night...

he looked back, and smiled, giving her a nod to continue on with dust's material...

dorothy nodded back, turned to the people and smiled...

they smiled politely, but starting getting a little restless...

dorothy decided to take a page from watchman's delivery by just stating the titles and moving on...

but before she did, dorothy looked down at the pages in front of her, looked back up at the people, and simply...and sincerely...said...

"trust me..."

...this one is mine...
—

open the machine

no rust to leave

brimming thirst to quench

a heart full of forgiveness

sanctuary refills

tap the water supply

no time to die

no rust to leave

time to open

the machine

...xtra marx...
—

fox crawls...
thru the wooded forest slowly

night falls...
but it leaves the light on boldly

sounds echo...
off trees that seem to be well placed, and

shepherds go...
and as far as i know, still wait...

river flows...
there's a babbling brook in the distance, and

heaven knows...
what the beauty of it all is

voices whispered...
yet still they follow trails untold

hearts are splintered...
and they seem to just grow old...

and the night can seem so cold...

...ain't dead yet...

—

i don't know...i'm not that sure...what is it
everyone is looking for
doesn't seem to be here...or perhaps it's right in
front of our faces
in one of these places...

people sing, people shout...people whisper till the
lights go out
the streets are full...but can the laughter stir the cry
dying just to live to die...

no chance at catching a breath...lungs are all
stuffed with
someone else's intent
eyes closed to realize...that something else rocked
my soul
'cause i still need that roll...

...bowery kids row...

—

under the fire escape
it's gettin' late
behind the condemned old picture show
they're hangin' out
that's what life's all about
for the kids who were all let go

starin' at the bricks
of the walls that stick
like mortar to their inner lives
city ain't a playground
livin' underground
where the only ones to count on, already died

'cause lives...don't cost too much
when the ice...hits the skids
and the night...takes to the slidin'
sunset on the bowery kids

open their eyes
a new day risin'
in this broken paradise
nothing to look for
nothing to hope for
nothing to sacrifice

breathin' in
coal from their sin
desolation on an empty shelf
there's no use wondrin'
there's no help comin'
not even from themselves

'cause lives...don't really matter
when night is shadowed...across their lids
no view in sight...only sunsets tonight
slidin' on the bowery kids...

as the sun sets on the bowery kids

...jerky...

—

i was speaking with jerky today...he told me that god showed him something last night...

he said, in his dream, he was in the parking lot at the back of a mall, and that he ran around the front, and then into one of the stores...

and...as he was going thru the sliding doors, he saw an elderly woman sitting on a bench, and a ten dollar bill lying on the floor in front of her, that he just knew that she dropped by accident, even though he didn't see her drop it...

and...he knew that a young man was going to walk thru the door, slip on the bill, and the elderly woman would, eventually, end up introducing the young man to her unmarried daughter, and the two would end up together...

so...he picked up the bill, handed it to the elderly woman, described the young man that would have slipped on it, and told her to simply stop him instead and save him the fall...

and...that was it...

yea...jerky is like that...he has these things, but i don't think we've ever been able to help him figure one out yet...

personally, i think he should write for television...

...one...

—

one drop...

hanging on to the leaf of

one tree...

growing up from the ground in

one spot...

giving shade on a sunny day to

one soul...

whose spirit is lifted for

one moment...

by the refreshing of the letting go of

one drop...

...subway evening news...

—

joey got home and clutched his chest
over stress that he goes thru
candy's still waitin' down by the gate
for a friend to throw a dollar or two
jimmy and timmy are talkin' over business
and the people they love to hate
while the little rockstar plays her steel guitar
to a song i can relate to...thru and thru...
like subway evening news
    never saw shoes that didn't look worn
    at least that's what the prophet said
    never had money, at least not enough
    and if i did, i just forget
    but i got a view from down in the tube
    of a light that's way past dawn
    flashing on thorns that won't draw blood
    i believe that stain's all gone...in the tomb...
    like subway evening news...
bobby left home when he was eleven, and
no one came looking for him
karen left town to find her crown
but she's gonna hafta start again
someone's still peein' on the side of the road
leaning up against the wall
shoe-shine salesman scratchin' his head
did you see what i just saw...in these shoes...
looked like subway evening news...

skirts are pretty this time in the city
when the wind blows them up in the air
some feel ashamed and some smile again
and some continue not to care
me, i never get time for time
that i need to get things done
but i'm always lookin' down the subway line
for the life that has begun
taking away every single day
with their own damn point of view
beautiful thing in this beautiful dream is
i got my own damn too...point of view...
like that subway evening news...

...socket to me...

—

the plug was in the socket today

...

it hasn't been for awhile

...

and when it is

...

we usually kick it out

...

not on purpose

...

not by accident

...

just because

...

...walkin' with the almost...

—

how can you fly
when you just keep on falling
how can you live
when your life
keeps on stalling

and how can you dream
with no angels around you
what is it that found you
lying there

how can you breathe
when your world's been depleted
and how can you see
when your know
you're not needed

and how can you laugh
when your tears fill the sewers
what are you doing
lying there

how can you speak
when the phone isn't ringing
and how can your week
spend another day repeating

and how can you suffer
with your blessings abundant
you've become so redundant
lying there

how can you fly…still you have to try…

...like a warm mug on a cold day...

—

god is watching me...

i can tell sometimes, ya' know...

i think he likes me...

i just get that feeling...

i know he looks out for me...

and i know he will when the time comes...

'cause i think he likes me...

i hope so...

i could be wrong...

but i don't think so...

...catbone dance...

—

if a black cat is supposed to be bad luck...

is a white cat supposed to be good...

i saw one today, cross my path

with the bluest of eyes

that glistened and shined...

she looked directly at me...

into me...

like she was trying to tell me something...

i pray it was good...

...tin toy box...

—

the melody plays, as dear old jack awaits
in the box
the handle is cranked, but inside it is dank
in the box

and it goes
up and down...up and down...
round and round...and round...

the song gets so tedious, just like a dream, it keeps
coming
from the box...
each minute left hoping, that jack will pop open
from the box...

as it goes
round and round...round and round...
up and down...and down...

round and round...round and round...
up and down...

and jack still awaits in his crouched up position
his heart beating as much as our anticipation
that we somehow find amusing...somehow find so
blind...
only to continue, when it's thru, we must rewind...

up and down…round and round…
up and down…round and round…
…and round…

...ashes to roses...

—

somedays...will never be the same
kick up your heels in the old driveway
and you go, thinking that the day is long, but
little did you know, you're not that strong

and it goes and it goes and it goes and it goes
taking you from ashes to roses
and you stall and you stall, and you try not to fall
covered up supposes...

one day...you're gonna learn a lesson
pick up your grip, and hold on tight
and when you go, you'll have no direction, but
one day soon you just might

and you'll go and you'll go and you'll go and you'll go
somewhere from ashes to roses
and you fly and you'll fly trying not to get too high
melted wing proposes

so it goes, so it goes, so it goes so it goes
holding on from ashes to roses
and you try and you try, 'cause you can't let it die
one door opens, another one closes

somewhere from ashes to roses...

...rag jaw boned...

—

separated...

like a moth behind glass

thru a window that won't open...

no collective breath

decidedly so...

kept apart

though strictly apart...

kept from touching

kept from being touched...

this rag jaw feeling

left incomplete...

not allowed

to fill its need...

close your eyes

it's time to rest...

...standing between speakers...

—

last seen on 14th street

called but no reply

the angel getting closer

to hear her last goodbye

the stage was set and lifted

to one casual exclaim

afraid she couldn't hear it

but there's no one else to blame

distracted by the noises

and consumed by all the fire

tempted by the struggle

and relaxed upon a wire

cautioned in new reasonings

and stamped into the ground

between the speakers loudening

and deafening the crowd

...plead for the relief of the coolest warmth...

—

stuck in the ravine...secure just like a dream...
can't afford escape because i'll only find the
raping of my soul as it lays bleeding...
and my heart...my heart dares to plead for your
arms around me
for i cannot see the fire or be free to live thru my desire...
and i can't express these feelings undefined
within my mind,
though they are written here within these pages...
but not in your arms...there's a separating while
i'm busy
rearranging all the terror in this firma that i need to
heed the warning, 'cause the truth is always hiding
'round the corner where i'm lying...
dying...to be...
in your
arms...

...keep the peas...

—

he sat at the table, holding his knife and fork, pushing his peas around

on his plate...

from the pitchest dark opening in the corner of the room, a female figure

dressed in powder blue came dancing out from the wall...

it distracted and stunned him for a moment, and, within an instant, he

noticed behind him a black-and-white film of old-time times square, filled

with raging amounts of joyous people...

he too had become black-and-white, not quite sure, not knowing, but

still quite sure...

he recognized it in a heartbeat, like a ticker-tape parade...

he couldn't connect with it, yet he was a part of it...

he leaned to his right, and his head dropped like a stone, and rose just

as quickly, to reveal, once again, his plate of peas...

...vestibule...

—

blackbird flies overhead

over hallowed ground

his wind on current

his wings specific

his flight determined

spiraling thru the tears and the smiles

the lies that beget all lies

lies within his presence

...see shell...

—

such beautiful strength...

such graceful love...

so present in all ages...

so sincere...so amazing...

like a tree that can bend

with the willowy breeze...

standing tall with roots

firmly placed within the strands of waterfall

that gently sway...

with eyes so deep as

the centre of light...

so understanding...and waiting...

a soul captivated within

such beautiful strength...

...sigh red one...

—

once was bitten...twice was shy
temptation lifted, but it still catches your eye
as the crimson wave creates
a perfect frame inside your mind
your breath is hardly breathing, but your heart, it
beats in time

    paperbag...left all alone
    no one to fill it up, nobody is at home
    as you stroll down to the marketplace
    without a point of view
    and suddenly it hits you, and you don't know
    what to do

        siren's echo...inside your fertile mind
        images are frozen, and you've chosen to be blind
        'cause the coral implications
        can't be bothered at this time
        imagination drifts inside the danger of the tide

    setting sail...no recourse
    following a dream that seems to have its own
    reward
    and then you shuffle in the distance
    creating what you see
    the veil has now been lifted, but you just can't
    seem to leave

pulling in...no pulling out
centrifugal deliverance leaves little in your doubt
as your bow breaks on the shoreline
splinters everywhere
the rocks have all been jagged, but you still don't
seem to care

body broken...left for dead
and still the thoughts are running deep inside your head
as the paperbag drifts off to find
another empty sea
your breath is barely breathing, but inside there's
still the need...

...holy ghostly...

—

this gig is so important...

together...you and me...

obscured by the world...

but not within each other...

return...reward...

the gift...the message...

let it leak, let it roll...

let it flood...

keep it coming...

no numbing or dumbing down...

no desperation...

love inspiration...

together...you and me...

this gig is so important...

...work in progress...

—

taking time to bless the day...

taking away what is said to be taken...

life precludes the sum of these parts...

and all the rest

merely shadows...

...shambolic...

—

rinse...repeat...

rinse...repeat...

when will it end

this redundancy

this formality

this cacophony

of anemic supposed-to-be's...

the wannabe's of things to come

that need for it to come...

rinse...repeat...

rinse...repeat...

...shallow fog rolling on an empty moor...

—

within the darkness, the machine is once again

woken up to another day, that will see it's final
end

total distraction, as anybody's guess

the ringing of the bell, that tells you all to rest

the truth is eminent, the tidal wave has shown

the hope of the innocent, and light years that
have flown

within the apologies, of the world outside your
door

this is the over now, that we have waited for...

...it hurts me too...

—

and with that, dorothy paused, leaving the last words of dust clinging in the air...

she looked at the faces of those still in attendance... and then she looked at watchman...

in his eyes she saw what was in her heart at that moment...but they were both satisfied...

the only thing left now was to thank the remaining crowd and go home...

as dorothy packed up her stuff, she gave jazz one last call...

he was groggy from some medication he took, but, fortunately, they said he was gonna be fine by morning...

dorothy took one look at watchman and concurred...”...aren't we all...”

watchman, feeling a little awkward at this moment, gave dorothy a hug nonetheless, while saying 'thank you' in his own gentle spirit...

dorothy, with a feeling of welcome in her own soul, grinned a little, while simply saying…

"hey…time to go home…you better follow me…"

...sweet home brownstone...

—

watchman, tired and a bit confused, followed dorothy, assuming she thought it would be safer that way...

when she got to her building, she turned around and placed something in watchman's hand...

he looked down and saw that it was a key...

dorothy, in her inimitable way, said..."now don't lose that or my landlady will kill me..."

still not grasping the situation a hundred percent, watchman wondered what dorothy had in mind...

at first, he perhaps thought, that it was an extra key to her apartment, and she was letting him stay the night...but dorothy spoke up to keep his confusion to a minimum...

"listen...it ain't much but...there's an attic space above my apartment...i spoke with my landlady and told her your situation...she's cool with it and isn't asking much money, so..."

watchman was about to interrupt her, but she continued on...

"yes…i know, don't worry…i'll be taking care of the rent for you…at least for now…but when your book hits the top of the new york times best seller list, then you can pay for mine as well…"

she laughed, putting watchman a little more at ease…

but…still seeing his trepidation, she quickly turned around, before he could change her mind, and opened the front door with the words…

"…now get inside ya' mook, before ya' let all the cold air in…and be careful on that ladder going up and down…i don't want another one of you in the hospital…"

watchman closed his eyes and followed her in, as the door closed behind…

...epilogue...

...again...

—

inverted daydreams cast shadows that hide away
the subtle changes of the morning...

and the breath on which you hold solid ground
cannot be found without revealing your sources...

and all the lambs that lay down are soon around
the ever-present thunder that rolls under the
keyboard and down
by the wayside...

and humanity is stricken once again...to placate
and evacuate as long as there's still time...

but who knows where is there or when...

and who will again...

...barricade...

—

got a coin in my hand that i flip thru my fingers
an old stogie who's smoke, in the air finally lingers
as i take a breath, and wonder, if it's my last

got a pen in my hand, that's been there since last thursday
an old cup of joe, straight black like it's s'possed to be
and everyone watching to see, if i will pass

doctors keep their distance
they don't want the headache now
of putting back the pieces
that only soul's rust will allow
corrective hindsight vision fills
the place with atmosphere
but nothing will be left, the moment
...that i leave here

got a thought in my head and i'm writing it down
tilting my head, so in coffee, i'll drown
goin' down for third time, in the last minute or so
while everyone wonders, if it's, my time to go

got a beat in my heart when i think of you
even though i know, that none of it's true
i still hold onto memories, even ones that i just made
it's all a point of questioning, when will my bill be paid

and morticians keep their eyes clear
just to see if i will fall
they'll catch me and they'll take me
to my final resting call
a little fire, a little smoke
open up that coffee can
throw my ashes in the deep end
then close lid again

...part in parcel...

—

...and the hope of the redundant, is easily revealed

for the truth of the temptation is the station's way
to feel

as the process of elimination carries its own wave

for the final destination is the cave...

...